Rodney Dunn grew up on a farm in rural New South Wales. During his chef apprenticeship he worked under Tetsuya Wakuda at esteemed Sydney restaurant Tetsuya's, before moving into food media. He has since developed recipes for most of Australia's food magazines and worked as food researcher for the *Better Homes and Gardens* television program. In 2004 he joined *Australian Gourmet Traveller* as food editor, and continued in the role of contributing food editor for the next 11 years.

A natural teacher, Rodney has taught cooking classes for Sydney Seafood School and Simon Johnson, but ultimately his passion for flavour led him to the land, and in 2007 he moved to Tasmania with his family to establish The Agrarian Kitchen.

theagrariankitchen.com

For Séverine, Tristan and the future little miss –
may our lives be filled with agrarian adventures together.

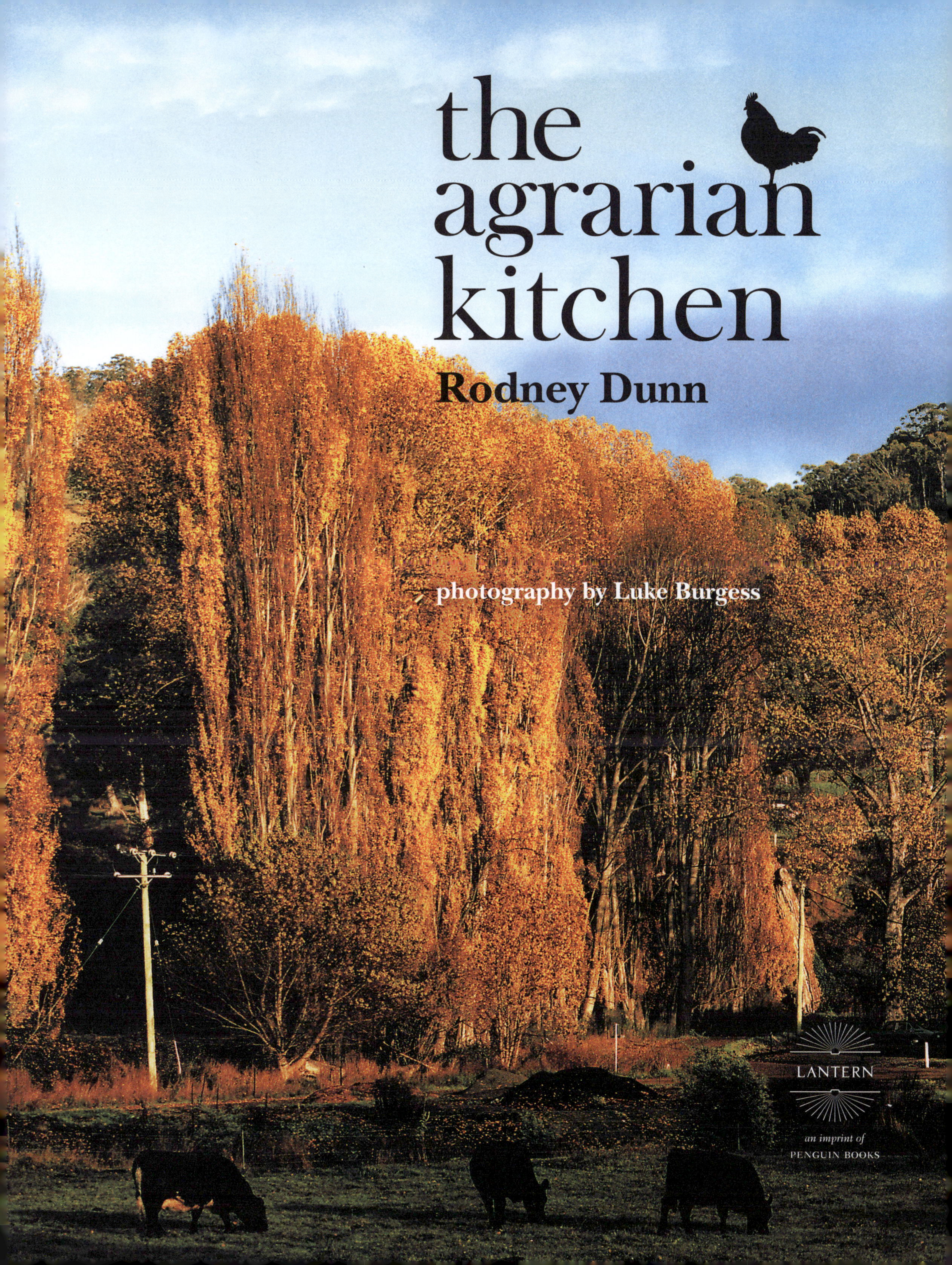

the agrarian kitchen

Rodney Dunn

photography by Luke Burgess

LANTERN

an imprint of
PENGUIN BOOKS

My search for a renewed connection with the food we eat took me
from inner-city Sydney to a misty valley in Tasmania.

Introduction

◇◇

If, like me, you are obsessed with food, you will attest to the eternal quest to enrich your life with amazing eating experiences. While I could blame my crazy idea of moving to the country on watching too much of Hugh Fearnley-Whittingstall's River Cottage television series, or reading the writings of Alice Waters and Paul Bertolli in the Chez Panisse cookbooks, somewhere along the way I had an epiphany. It dawned on me that the majority of the food I was eating in restaurants was days, sometimes weeks or even months old, the product of an industrial farming system that values high yields and amenability to transport and storage above flavour. Remember that as soon as something is harvested, it begins to deteriorate, so I realised that if I wanted to experience a fruit or vegetable at its best, I needed to get as close to that point as possible.

Ironically, I grew up in the country, but as a teenager all I ever wanted to do was head to the city, because I thought that's where it was all happening – the bright lights, the bustling restaurants – and by then I had my heart set on becoming a chef. I have heard it said that to be a good cook, first you have to be a good eater, and as a young lad it seemed I was always hungry; hollow legs, I think they called it! The other career inkling I had was teaching. However, I felt I could always go back to university if this cooking thing didn't work out. Life has such a funny way of making things happen that one would have never thought possible, such as combining the two.

After beginning my chef apprenticeship in Griffith in south-east New South Wales, I found my way to the kitchen of Sam Vico at Caffe Bassano. It was here that I learnt to cook Italian food with heart, to cook seasonally and simply, honouring the ingredient. In the last year of my apprenticeship, at the age of twenty, I left for Sydney to work for Tetsuya Wakuda at his restaurant, which was then in the inner-western suburb of Rozelle. At the time, I didn't realise the impact this would have on the rest of my life. We worked long, hard hours in a small kitchen, and faced a whole new level of expectation and discipline – an experience that has held me in good stead ever since. Of course, there was also the opportunity to sample some amazing produce: I will never forget the time a box of white Alba truffles arrived straight from the airport, or the summertime crates of farm-fresh white peaches that drove everyone crazy with their sweet, luscious fragrance.

In that same kitchen I met one of my best mates, Luke Burgess. Like me, Luke was an apprentice chef, and we bonded on the first day, forging a friendship that has stayed the distance across career paths and states. He even introduced me to the love of my life, Séverine. To this day, Luke still influences the way I cook and is a constant sounding board for advice.

He has also taken all the photos for this book, capturing our daily life at The Agrarian Kitchen in a way only he could.

It was during a two-week break from Tetsuya's that I had the opportunity to spend some time assisting a food photographer. A whole new world opened before my eyes, one in which I could satisfy my two passions, food and books. (Those of you who have visited The Agrarian Kitchen will know that my passion for cookbooks is definitely bordering on obsession!) Over the next seven years I worked on a freelance basis, cooking for photo shoots and television shows, and writing some of my own recipes for food magazines.

In 2004 Séverine and I got married, and after our honeymoon I started at *Australian Gourmet Traveller*. For three years I held the enviable position of food editor at the magazine, working with a team of talented people to create recipes for its glossy pages, a job that for many would have been the pinnacle of a career. I, however, was quietly developing the notion of moving to Tasmania, the only slight flaw in the plan being that I had never actually been there . . . Fortuitously, Tourism Tasmania extended an invitation for someone from the magazine to attend their Ten Days on the Island festival, and of course I jumped at the chance. When I got there, I was as wide-eyed as a kid in a candy store: I spoke to chefs who told me stories of abundant wild food foraged from forests and hedgerows, and sampled produce grown and raised in the purest air in the world. If moving to Tasmania had been just a dream up until then, after that brief visit it became a mission.

It took a few years of on-and-off searching with a few false starts before we found the right place, and we had almost given up hope when the Old Schoolhouse at Lachlan came up. I guess I had an image in my mind of the setting I wanted for our new life, and the closer I got, the more boxes I was ticking off. The village of Lachlan is nestled in a valley, with hills rising up on all sides like an amphitheatre. The property itself is surrounded by mature deciduous trees – elms, oaks and poplars – and, given it was autumn, their leaves painted the ground golden. The house sat in the middle of five acres, somewhat smaller than I was initially after, but I was won over by how perfect the building was. Like all country schools built around that time (Lachlan school dates from 1887), it consisted of two main parts, the school rooms and the headmaster's residence. The old classrooms had been divided by a wall with a large sliding door and the light streamed in through huge banks of windows at either end. My mind was working overtime as I stood and stared out of the kitchen windows to the mountains beyond. Could I imagine people cooking in here? Armed with photos and video footage, I returned to Sydney intent on convincing Séverine that this was the place for us.

Several months later, we bought the warmest woollen doona we could lay our hands on and set about moving to one of the coldest parts of Australia in the middle of winter. It didn't take us long to understand that heating was a necessity. We burnt through our first tonne of firewood in about a week before we realised we didn't need to keep three fires burning.

Wisely, Séverine talked me out of the idea of a restaurant, and between us we evolved the idea of a farm-based cooking school.

Five years on, our farm now includes pigs, chickens, goats and a flock of geese, as well as an extensive vegetable garden, orchard, berry patch and herb garden.

Anyone with an old house will empathise, for they are impossible to keep warm. Our kitchen floor had updrafts that would rival the latest-model air conditioner; as we huddled around the open fire, our toes were being blasted by Antarctic winds that whistled through the floorboards. For the next two months, apart from keeping warm, Séverine and I spent our evenings putting together a submission for a government-sponsored tourism promotion grant we had found out about. Each night we put our four-month-old son Tristan to bed and beavered away into the wee hours, laying our dream onto paper in order to convince other people this thing had legs – and ourselves that we were not totally crazy.

By early 2008 we had eaten into most of our savings, and things were looking a little dire as we anxiously awaited the outcome of our submission. When we finally heard that our application had been successful, it felt like winning the lottery! Over the next nine months, the small domestic kitchen was removed, the floorboards were replaced and the classrooms re-painted from top to bottom, then a wood-fired oven and a new commercial kitchen were installed. And that was just the inside. Outside, a car park was constructed and a paddock was transformed into the beginnings of a garden.

We officially opened in November 2008, and it all went smoothly, even with the haphazard charm that tends to accompany the first day of any new venture. During our first year of operation, it was just the two of us: I would teach the class and Séverine would wash up, in between caring for Tristan. She would put him down for a sleep in time to help serve the meal and pour the wine. If we were lucky, he would sleep through until the end of class . . . and then be wide awake until much later at night, but we figured it was a small price to pay.

On my arrival here, I was a complete novice when it came to the nitty-gritty of actually growing things. I was, to quote my father, 'green behind the ears'. Well, as it turns out, all I really needed to do was to get the green from behind my ears and into my thumbs. At a time when so many of us yearn for a more meaningful connection with the natural world, I like to think that what we are offering is a taste of the very nourishing experience of tending a garden and raising animals. For me, The Agrarian Kitchen represents the chance to share the simple pleasures of cooking and eating in tune with the seasons, and the rewards of a life lived close to the earth.

— chapter one —

spring

WILD GREENS . ARTICHOKES
CHEESE-MAKING . PICNICS
ELDERFLOWERS

Spring, as the old adage has it, is a time of new birth, a fresh start. But those who are connected to the land know it is also the busiest and most crucial time if the growing season ahead is to be plentiful. I am choosing to start the chapters of this book here because, for us, it marks the beginning of our gardening year.

It is also a season full of hope . . . hope that all the hard work of planting will reap rewards; hope that the frost will not freeze the fruit blossom and hinder the harvest. Most importantly, hope that the summer ahead will be long and warm, to allow our crops to thrive.

Smoked ham and watercress soup

Serves 6

Each spring the watercourses around The Agrarian Kitchen come alive with dense beds of peppery wild watercress. Paired with smoky, briny morsels of ham hock and the fresh flavour of mint, the vibrant mustard like hit of watercress is what this soup is all about.

1 smoked ham hock (about 600 g)
2 carrots, coarsely chopped
2 brown onions, coarsely chopped
1 stalk celery, coarsely chopped
1 tablespoon black peppercorns
3 bay leaves
4 cloves garlic, bruised
5 sprigs thyme
125 g shelled peas (from about 300 g peas in pods)
300 g watercress, trimmed
sea salt and freshly ground black pepper
mint leaves, to serve

In a large saucepan or stockpot, combine ham hock, carrot, onion, celery, peppercorns, bay leaves, garlic and thyme. Cover with 5 litres water and bring to the boil over high heat. Using a slotted spoon, skim and discard any scum that rises to the surface.

Reduce heat until broth simmers gently and cook until ham is falling from the bone, about 3 hours. Remove hock from broth and set aside on a plate to cool slightly.

Strain broth through a sieve, reserving liquid and discarding solids. Return broth to the rinsed-out pan.

Shred meat from ham hock, discarding any fat and tendons and the bone. Return ham to broth and add peas and watercress. Season with salt and pepper and allow watercress to just wilt in the heat of the broth.

Serve immediately, scattered with freshly torn mint leaves.

Ricotta and quail egg ravioli

Serves 4

If quail eggs prove tricky to find, you can substitute hen eggs, which also means you will have a little more leeway with the cooking time. What you are aiming for is to cook the ravioli just long enough for the pasta to be tender, leaving the egg yolk runny so it oozes out when the ravioli is cut and mingles with the sauce.

350 g firm ricotta, drained (see page 16)
1 egg, beaten, plus extra for egg wash
2 cloves garlic, finely chopped
80 g (1 cup) finely grated parmesan
sea salt and freshly ground black pepper
16 quail eggs

pasta dough
300 g (2 cups) plain flour
2 eggs

zucchini, pea and mint burnt butter
150 g unsalted butter
4 cloves garlic, thinly sliced
1 zucchini (courgette), halved lengthways and sliced
70 g (about ½ cup) shelled peas (from approximately 175 g peas in pods)
2 tablespoons mint leaves, torn
sea salt and freshly ground black pepper

For pasta dough, place flour in a large bowl. Make a well in the centre, add eggs and 1–2 tablespoons cold water then gradually incorporate flour into eggs, working with a fork and then your hands until dough just comes together. Turn out onto a lightly floured work surface and knead until smooth. Wrap in plastic film and set aside to rest at room temperature for at least 1 hour (the dough can be refrigerated for up to 24 hours – just bring it back to room temperature before rolling).

Meanwhile, using the back of a large metal spoon, press ricotta through a coarse sieve into a bowl. Add beaten egg, garlic and parmesan and mix to combine. Season with salt and pepper, then refrigerate until required.

Divide pasta dough into four and work with one piece at a time, keeping the other pieces covered. Using a pasta machine with rollers set at their widest setting, feed dough through rollers. Fold dough in half lengthways, then feed through rollers again and continue until dough is smooth and silky. Now keep rolling the dough, reducing the setting of the rollers each time, until pasta sheets are translucent and 1 mm thick. Cut pasta into sheets about 40 cm long, scatter with semolina or flour and lay on a clean work surface, overlapping them slightly. To prevent pasta sheets from drying out, cover them with a clean tea towel, then with a damp tea towel.

Place a sheet of pasta on a clean work surface and cut into 10 cm squares. Spoon 1 tablespoon of filling onto each square and make an indentation in the centre. Separate a quail egg and gently slip the yolk into the hollow. Brush the edges of the pasta with egg, place another square on top and press edges to seal, taking care to squeeze out any air. Repeat with remaining pasta, filling and quail eggs to make 16 ravioli.

Cook the ravioli a few at a time in a large saucepan of simmering salted water until the pasta is just cooked (1–2 minutes), then remove using a slotted spoon.

Meanwhile, for zucchini, pea and mint burnt butter, melt butter in a large frying pan over medium heat, add garlic and zucchini and sauté until nut-brown (4–5 minutes). Add peas and cook until tender (about 2–3 minutes), then stir through mint and season with salt and pepper.

When all the ravioli is cooked, add to the burnt butter and carefully toss to combine. Serve immediately, drizzled with plenty of burnt butter.

Making ricotta

◇◇◇

Makes about 1 kg

More often than not we will make ricotta in Agrarian Kitchen classes: it is straightforward and easy to do, and is one of the quickest and most gratifying ways to use surplus milk. The class first milks our goats then turns that milk into ricotta, which is transformed into a dish for lunch. Many people find it quite surreal to think that what they're eating was inside a goat's udder only hours ago!

While I would encourage owning a goat, I realise this is not always practical, so feel free to use good-quality organic full-cream cow's milk instead. If you have some milk in the fridge that you won't get to use, turn it into ricotta and it will keep for several days – just reduce the amount of vinegar proportionately to the amount of milk.

In fact, I usually don't measure the vinegar, instead just adding a little at a time and removing the curds that form after each addition. If the milk is still white, reheat the milk to 90°C, add a little more vinegar and skim off the curds until there is only clear yellow-ish whey left in the pan. (The same effect can be achieved with lemon juice.) The gradual addition of the vinegar allows for variations in the acidity of different vinegars and means you will always end up with soft, creamy curd.

5 litres milk (cow's, sheep's or goat's milk can be used)
60 ml (¼ cup) white vinegar

Heat milk in a large saucepan or stockpot over low heat until temperature reaches 90–95°C.

Quickly stir in vinegar and, using a slotted spoon, remove curds as they rise to the surface and transfer to a muslin-lined colander set over a bowl. Leave to drain for about 10 minutes.

Place ricotta in an airtight container and refrigerate until required. It will keep well for 3–4 days in the fridge.

Note
The other great thing about making your own ricotta is that you can adjust the moisture content to suit your preference and how you want to use the ricotta. For pasta fillings, drier ricotta works better, but if you like a moister ricotta for eating fresh, just add a little whey to the ricotta container before refrigerating.

Draining ricotta. For firm ricotta, simply leave it to drain a little longer.

Wild greens and prosciutto omelette

Serves 2

Omelettes are our go-to dish for lunch or dinner when we have been too busy to organise something more substantial. Of course the filling can be varied, but beware: an omelette should not be a dumping ground for the contents of the fridge! A good omelette needs to be a considered compilation. When cooked to perfection – barely set with a still-creamy centre – an omelette can be proudly served to even the most discerning diner on any occasion.

5 eggs
150 ml pouring cream
sea salt and freshly ground black pepper
50 g unsalted butter
2 cloves garlic, very thinly sliced
50 g wild greens (such as fat hen, nettles, dandelion leaves, chickweed, wild rocket, baby spinach), washed
30 g thinly sliced prosciutto

Combine eggs and cream in a small bowl and whisk until just combined. Season lightly with salt and pepper.

Heat a 20 cm frying pan over medium heat, add butter and cook until frothy. Add beaten eggs and, using a fork, drag the set outer edges into the centre, working around the pan until the base of the omelette is just set.

Scatter over sliced garlic, greens and prosciutto then, using a spatula, carefully fold omelette in half, slide onto a plate and serve immediately. The omelette can either be split in half or shared from the same plate.

Fried artichokes and spring vegetables with béarnaise sauce

Serves 4

This dish only has the desired effect if it's made with the freshest vegetables. Then, it is a celebration of spring, combining all that is good from the garden with the other wonder of the season – eggs. Yes, there are eggs available for most of the year, but they are at their most abundant in spring. The béarnaise sauce is technically a hollandaise with tarragon, but you can substitute whatever is available in your herb garden or greengrocer.

This way of frying artichokes is traditionally associated with the Jewish quarter of Rome, and it gives them a beautifully nutty flavour. Unfortunately, artichokes are often overlooked by home cooks, who are intimidated by their seemingly complicated preparation. But it's really not that tricky: if you want to know what bits to peel off and which to leave on, check out the step-by-step guide on page 23.

12 globe artichokes
squeeze of lemon juice
1.5 litres olive oil, for deep-frying
sea salt
300 g broccoli, broken into small florets
24 asparagus spears, trimmed
24 baby radishes

béarnaise sauce
75 ml white wine vinegar
75 ml white wine
2 golden shallots, thinly sliced
10 black peppercorns
3 egg yolks
200 ml clarified butter
sea salt and freshly ground black pepper
1 tablespoon finely chopped tarragon

For béarnaise sauce, combine vinegar, wine, shallots and peppercorns in a saucepan. Simmer over medium heat until reduced by half, then strain into a heatproof bowl. Add egg yolks and whisk over a saucepan of gently simmering water until pale and frothy and thick enough to hold a ribbon when drizzled from the whisk. Remove from heat and gradually whisk in butter. Season with salt and pepper, then stir in tarragon.

Prepare artichokes by removing outer leaves and trimming top. Peel artichoke stalks. Halve artichokes lengthways and, using a teaspoon, remove hairy choke. Place artichokes in a bowl of water acidulated with lemon juice. Heat oil in a large, deep saucepan to 180°C. Drain artichokes and pat dry with paper towel. Deep-fry until golden and tender, about 2–3 minutes, then drain on paper towel and sprinkle with salt.

Blanch broccoli and asparagus in a large saucepan of boiling salted water for 1 minute, then drain well.

To serve, arrange artichokes and other vegetables on a platter with béarnaise sauce on the side.

Note
To clarify butter, cut into chunks and slowly melt in a saucepan over low heat. Using a slotted spoon, skim scum from surface and discard, then carefully pour off the clear, golden liquid butter, leaving behind the white milk solids in the base of the pan. Discard milk solids. The clarified butter is now ready to use. Any leftover clarified butter can be kept, refrigerated in an airtight container, for a couple of months.

Globe artichokes are an architectural statement in the garden,
and a welcome harbinger of spring in the kitchen.

Step-by-step guide to preparing globe artichokes

◇◇◇

1

Prepare artichokes by removing outer leaves. Remove enough leaves to expose a lemon-yellow ring around the base of the artichoke.

2

Peel artichoke stalks. You will need a sharp knife. Starting at the base, trim down along the stalk, cleaning the stringy outer layer of the stalk and the knobbly bits where the outer leaves have been removed.

3

Trim top. Square off the top of the artichoke, as these leaves are tough and stringy.

4

Halve artichokes lengthways. Halving the artichoke allows you to see the choke and remove it.

5

Using a teaspoon, remove the hairy choke. The choke is the beginning of the flower's stamen, so the size of the choke will increase as the flower develops. When an artichoke appears on the plant, pick it as soon as possible, then there may be little or no choke to remove.

6

Place artichokes in a bowl of water acidulated with lemon juice. As soon as the flesh of the artichoke is exposed to air it begins to oxidise and turn black. Prepare one artichoke at a time, from start to finish, and place it in the acidulated water before starting the next.

Smoked eel with kohlrabi rémoulade and horseradish

Serves 4 as a starter

In this country eel is one of the most underrated fish; perhaps it's the slipperiness that makes people squeamish. Skinned and cooked, though, their rich flesh is divine – particularly when smoked. You should be able to find smoked eel at good fishmongers and specialist food stores. If you can't get fresh horseradish, just leave it out; the bottled stuff would be too vinegary here. This dish makes a perfect starter, and a good excuse to use kohlrabi, which let's face it looks like something from outer space!

800 g smoked eel, cut into four portions
1 small cucumber
5 cm piece of horseradish, peeled
chive flowers, to serve (optional)

kohlrabi rémoulade
500 g kohlrabi, peeled
2 egg yolks
1 tablespoon lemon juice
2 teaspoons dijon mustard
200 ml grapeseed oil
sea salt and freshly ground black pepper
large handful mixed herbs, such as coriander, mint, basil, chervil, tarragon and parsley

For kohlrabi rémoulade, using a mandoline with a comb attachment or a coarse grater, finely shred kohlrabi. Place egg yolks, lemon juice and mustard in the bowl of a food processor or blender and process until mixture is pale and fluffy. With motor running, add oil in a thin steady stream until mayonnaise is thick and emulsified, then season with salt and pepper. Combine mayonnaise, kohlrabi and herbs and refrigerate until required – leaving it to stand for at least 1 hour will allow the flavours to combine.

Meanwhile, using a sharp knife, cut fillets from the eel and remove and discard skin. Cover loosely and set aside for about an hour to warm to room temperature.

Peel cucumber and, using a mandoline or swivel peeler, shave into ribbons.

To serve, place kohlrabi rémoulade and cucumber onto plates and top with eel. Finely grate over some horseradish and scatter with chive flowers, if using.

The smokehouse

The decision to build our smokehouse arose from the desire to produce our own smoked hams and bacon. What we didn't anticipate was the new world this would open up for us to experiment with smoking other meats, fish, dairy products, fruit and vegetables.

Smoking is most prevalent in countries whose colder climates need a helping hand to dry meat or fish for preservation. In this time-honoured craft, animals fattened from the abundance of autumn were slaughtered and salted, then hung high in the fireplace chimney where cool smoke wafted over them, slowly drying out the meat and coating the outside in antibacterial smoke particles. This allowed meat to be kept over the winter months without refrigeration.

Only cold smoke (below 36°C) preserves; hot-smoking, although delicious, also cooks the meat or fish, which then needs to be consumed immediately or refrigerated. The cooler the smoke, the better the result. Maintaining a low temperature is also crucial for food-safety reasons, as warm smoke will promote the growth of bacteria. Commercial smokers cool the generated smoke, enabling their use year-round, but our rustic version means that smoking can only be done in cooler weather – effectively late autumn, all of winter and early spring.

Often mistaken at first glance for the outhouse, our smoker consists of a concrete firebox, which generates the smoke, and the smokehouse itself, which holds whatever is being smoked. The firebox sits slightly lower than the house and has a sliding metal door that controls the amount of air reaching the fire – the key to generating smoke is to allow the fire just enough air to slowly smoulder. The smoke travels along a concrete pipe into the middle of the smokehouse, where vents at the front and back draw the smoke evenly through the space.

Hardwoods are the smoking wood of choice, as softwoods tend to produce a bitter, acrid smoke. Heated debates rage over which wood is best, and we are constantly experimenting with local sources: we currently use the chipped prunings from our fruit trees and clean shavings of Tasmanian oak, myrtle and sassafras from a cabinetmaker friend.

Although the wonders of modern technology mean that smoking is no longer a necessity, the alluring flavours that tantalise and excite our tastebuds ensure its continuing popularity.

Pan-fried squid with broad beans and chorizo

Serves 4

When we use broad beans in class, it usually divides the crowd; people seem to either love or hate them. On closer investigation those who hate them have usually suffered through mealy and starchy broad beans that have been picked too late. To add insult to injury, the beans have then been boiled until they are grey and watery. Broad beans need to be picked young and sweet, like peas. At this size they can be eaten raw or just lightly blanched – and come with a proud track record of converting every hater I've come across into a lover. Well, let's say a liker . . .

300 g young broad beans (from about 800 g beans in pods)
500 g squid, cleaned, tentacles reserved
80 ml (⅓ cup) olive oil
6 cloves garlic, thinly sliced
100 g chorizo, cut into 1 cm pieces
3 strips lemon rind
sea salt and freshly ground black pepper
large handful mint leaves, coarsely torn
lemon wedges, to serve

Bring a large saucepan of salted water to the boil over high heat, add broad beans and cook for 1 minute, then drain in a sieve and refresh under cold running water.

Using a sharp knife, thinly slice squid tubes into strips about 5 cm long. Cut tentacles to separate each leg and set aside.

Heat olive oil in a large frying pan over medium–high heat, add garlic and sauté until fragrant, about 1 minute. Add squid and chorizo and sauté until squid is just cooked and beginning to colour. Add broad beans and lemon rind, then season with salt and pepper and cook until beans are just warmed through. Stir through mint leaves and serve immediately, with lemon wedges for squeezing.

Chargrilled quail with nettle and lovage cream

Serves 8

I find it very satisfying to use several products from the one animal in a single dish, such as pork served with lard-fried potatoes, or the quail and quail eggs in this dish. Quail eggs may look fragile and delicate but the shell is actually as strong, if not stronger, than that of hen eggs. If possible try to use slightly older eggs for boiling as the air sac inside will be larger, making them easier to peel. I find that giving them a tap on the base (the more rounded end) is a good way to get started, as this is where the air sac is; having a bowl of cold water on hand to rinse away fragments of shell also helps. I love using weeds – the ultimate gardener's revenge! Nettles are amazingly good for us: high in vitamins A, C and D, and with healthy amounts of iron and calcium – just make sure you wear gloves to handle them before they're cooked. Here they are blended with lovage in an extremely more-ish sauce. If you have time, marinate the quail overnight for the best flavour.

12 quail, halved
sea salt and freshly ground black pepper
16 quail eggs
60 ml (¼ cup) olive oil

garlic marinade
6 cloves garlic, peeled
2 handfuls flat-leaf parsley leaves
150 ml extra virgin olive oil

nettle and lovage cream
60 g unsalted butter
1 onion, finely chopped
3 cloves garlic
50 g nettle leaves (or, at a pinch, baby spinach)
150 ml milk
20 g lovage leaves (or celery leaves)
sea salt and freshly ground black pepper

pangrattato
120 g coarse fresh breadcrumbs
1 clove garlic, finely chopped
30 ml extra virgin olive oil

For garlic marinade, place garlic and parsley leaves into a small blender and process to a fine paste. Stir through olive oil.

Place quail in a large bowl and season well with salt and pepper. Pour over garlic marinade and rub into quail. Cover and refrigerate for between 1 and 24 hours.

For nettle and lovage cream, heat butter in a small saucepan over medium heat. Add onion and garlic and cook, stirring often, until caramelised, about 10 minutes. Add nettle leaves to saucepan and sauté until wilted, then add milk and simmer until reduced by two-thirds, about 5 minutes. Stir through lovage, then purée in a blender until smooth and season to taste.

Bring a saucepan of water to the boil, add quail eggs and cook for 2 minutes, then remove and immediately refresh in cold running water. Peel and set aside.

For pangrattato, preheat oven to 180°C. Combine all ingredients in a large bowl, then spread them out on a baking tray. Bake, stirring occasionally, until golden, about 10 minutes.

Preheat a chargrill pan or barbecue grillplate over high heat. Drizzle quail with olive oil and cook skin-side down until golden, about 2 minutes, then turn and continue to cook until just cooked through.

Serve quail on nettle and lovage cream with soft-boiled quail eggs and pangrattato.

Leg of lamb with basil stuffing

Serves 8

This basil stuffing is based on pesto and is quite versatile, so much so that I use it for everything from chicken to beef. A lamb leg is quite straightforward to debone, but if you have neither the will nor the time, feel free to ask your butcher. Be sure to leave the shank bone in, as the presentation is much nicer. You can also cook a lamb shoulder the same way, although you may want to give it longer in the oven.

1 × 3.3 kg leg of lamb, deboned (about 2.8 kg after deboning)
60 ml (¼ cup) olive oil

basil stuffing
2 tablespoons olive oil
2 brown onions, thinly sliced
sea salt and freshly ground black pepper
80 g basil leaves (about 1 bunch)
3 cloves garlic
50 g (⅓ cup) pine nuts
20 g (¼ cup) finely grated parmesan
100 ml extra virgin olive oil
140 g (2 cups) fresh breadcrumbs

For basil stuffing, heat olive oil in a frying pan over low heat, add onion and a pinch of salt and cook, stirring often, over low heat until caramelised, about 10 minutes. Set aside to cool. Meanwhile, place basil leaves, garlic and a pinch of salt in a mortar and, using a pestle, crush coarsely. Add pine nuts and parmesan and pound to a smooth paste, then stir through extra virgin olive oil and season with salt and pepper. Combine pesto, breadcrumbs and caramelised onion.

Place lamb skin-side down on a clean work surface and evenly spread stuffing over meat. Starting at one of the long sides, roll up and secure with kitchen twine.

Preheat oven to 200°C. Heat olive oil in a large heavy-based casserole, add lamb and cook over high heat, turning frequently, until golden brown, about 5–6 minutes. Cover, place in the oven and cook for 30 minutes, then reduce oven temperature to 160°C and cook for a further 40 minutes – this will result in medium-rare meat.

To serve, remove twine and cut lamb into 3 cm thick slices.

Poached strawberries with basil, goat's milk labneh and shortbread

Serves 4

Strawberries are the first of the berries for the season, and will fruit prolifically right through to the end of summer. They are easy to grow and even easier to eat – the difficult part is getting them from the strawberry patch to the kitchen. The trick with this recipe is not to cook the strawberries but just to let the warmth of the syrup intensify their sweetness, which makes a wonderful contrast to the aniseed flavour of the basil. Yoghurt goes perfectly with fruit, and draining out the excess moisture to make labneh gives an even creamier result.

300 g strawberries
220 g (1 cup) caster sugar
12 basil leaves

labneh
1 kg goat's milk yoghurt

shortbread
160 g plain flour
125 g unsalted butter, cut into 2 cm pieces
30 g caster sugar
sea salt
icing sugar, for dusting

To make labneh, spoon yoghurt into a muslin-lined sieve set over a bowl. Cover loosely and place in the refrigerator for 3–4 hours or until yoghurt has thickened.

For shortbread, place flour, butter, sugar and a pinch of salt in a large bowl and, using your fingertips, rub in butter until mixture resembles coarse breadcrumbs. Add 1 tablespoon iced water and gently knead until dough just comes together. Form dough into a flat disc, wrap in plastic film and refrigerate for about 1 hour.

Preheat oven to 180°C and line a baking tray with baking paper. On a lightly floured work surface, roll out shortbread dough to about 8 mm thick. Using a 5 cm diameter cutter, press out rounds of shortbread and place on prepared baking tray. Bake shortbread for 12–15 minutes or until golden. Remove to a wire rack to cool, then dust with icing sugar.

Hull strawberries and halve them lengthways. Combine sugar and 250 ml (1 cup) water in a non-reactive saucepan and stir over medium heat until sugar has dissolved. Add strawberries and basil leaves and stir to combine, then immediately remove from the heat and set aside until cooled to room temperature.

Serve strawberries with labneh and shortbread.

Goat's milk dulce de leche ice cream

Makes 1.8 litres

Dulce de leche must be one of the greatest flavours invented. Essentially a simple caramel made by reducing milk and sugar together, it is enough to send you weak at the knees. We often make it with our own goat's milk, but any full-cream milk can be used – it's always the first of our preserves to sell out. Most people find it hard to resist a spoonful straight from the jar, but it's also delicious folded through vanilla ice cream.

375 ml (1½ cups) goat's milk
450 ml pouring cream
1 vanilla bean, halved lengthways
8 egg yolks
150 g caster sugar

dulce de leche
1 litre goat's milk
220 g (1 cup) sugar
¼ teaspoon bicarbonate of soda
1 vanilla bean, halved lengthways and seeds scraped

To make dulce de leche, combine ingredients in a large saucepan. Bring to the boil over medium–high heat, then reduce heat until milk is gently simmering and cook, stirring often, until mixture has thickened and is dark caramel in colour, about 40 minutes. Allow to cool in saucepan, then transfer to an airtight container and refrigerate until required – dulce de leche will keep in the fridge for up to 1 month.

Place milk, cream and vanilla bean in a saucepan and bring to the boil. In a bowl, whisk egg yolks and sugar until thick and pale, then gradually whisk in hot milk. Return custard to same pan and stir over low heat until it thickens enough to coat the back of a wooden spoon – do not let it boil. Remove from heat and strain through a fine sieve into a bowl. Remove vanilla bean, scrape out seeds and stir into custard. Allow to cool slightly, then refrigerate until chilled.

Freeze custard in an ice-cream machine according to manufacturer's instructions. Remove from churn and gently fold in 375 ml (1½ cups) dulce de leche. Place ice cream in a container, cover and freeze until firm.

Brioche doughnuts with lemon curd and lavender sugar

Makes about 20

Simply baked, the dough for this brioche makes a lovely loaf, but when fried it produces the lightest, most divine doughnuts. The lemon curd offsets the richness of the doughnuts, and any left over is a handy thing for the fridge. Lavender is hardy, easy to grow and tolerates a wide range of climates; we usually collect the flowers from our garden once they have dried on the plant. If you are doing the same, ensure the flowers are completely dry before storing them in an airtight container in the spice cupboard. Too often relegated to the sock drawer or pot-pourri, lavender has relevance in the kitchen. As well as the beautifully scented sugar used here, it makes a sophisticated ice cream – just tread carefully as the flavour is strong and can be overpowering if too much is used.

110 g (½ cup) caster sugar
1 teaspoon dried lavender flowers
vegetable oil, for deep-frying

brioche
450 g (3 cups) plain flour
3 teaspoons dried yeast
2 tablespoons caster sugar
fine sea salt
60 ml (¼ cup) milk
4 eggs, lightly beaten
250 g soft unsalted butter, plus extra for greasing

lemon curd
2 eggs
4 egg yolks
125 ml (½ cup) lemon juice (from about 3–4 lemons), strained
110 g (½ cup) caster sugar
80 g unsalted butter, coarsely chopped

For brioche, combine flour, yeast, sugar and a pinch of salt in the bowl of an electric mixer fitted with a dough hook. Mix on low speed until combined then, with the motor running, add milk and beaten egg and mix until it just comes together. Add butter, a little at time, beating until each addition has been incorporated before adding the next, until dough is smooth and shiny. Transfer dough to a lightly greased bowl, cover and stand in a draught-free place for 1 hour or until doubled in size. Knock back dough, then leave stand for another hour or until doubled in size.

Meanwhile, to make lemon curd, lightly whisk eggs, egg yolks, lemon juice and sugar in a non-reactive saucepan. Place over low heat and stir continuously for 10 minutes or until mixture thickens enough to coat the back of a wooden spoon. Remove pan from heat and add butter piece by piece, stirring until smooth. Cover closely with plastic film and refrigerate. (Lemon curd will keep in the fridge for up to 3 days.)

For lavender sugar, combine caster sugar and lavender in a spice grinder or mortar and pestle and grind to a fine powder. Store in an airtight jar until required.

Heat vegetable oil in a large, deep saucepan or deep-fryer to 180°C and line a large plate with paper towel. Using two dessertspoons, scoop spoonfuls of dough into the hot oil and fry, in batches, for 2–3 minutes or until golden brown, then remove and drain on the paper-lined plate. Continue until all the dough is cooked.

To serve, roll warm doughnuts in lavender sugar and set aside to cool slightly. Using a serrated knife, split doughnuts in half and fill with lemon curd.

Lemon and elderflower sorbet

Makes about 1 litre

If you have never tried elderflowers, their taste is hard to describe – but if I had to give it a go, the word ethereal pops into mind. Once picked, the flowers fade quickly, so there is always a mad springtime rush to preserve their elusive flavour in cordials and syrups. Combined with citrus, elderflowers really sing.

220 g (1 cup) sugar
4 heads elderflower, plus extra to serve
rind of 1 lemon, peeled off in strips
1 tablespoon liquid glucose
150 ml lemon juice (from about 4–5 lemons)
sparkling wine, to serve

Combine sugar, elderflowers, lemon rind and 250 ml (1 cup) water in a non-reactive saucepan and stir over low heat until sugar has dissolved. Stir through glucose and lemon juice then remove from heat. Cover with a lid and set aside at room temperature for at least 30 minutes to allow elderflower flavour to infuse.

Strain mixture, discarding lemon rind and elderflowers, then chill until cold. Churn in an ice cream machine according to manufacturer's instructions.

Scoop sorbet into elegant glasses, pour over a little sparking wine, garnish with elderflowers and serve immediately.

Note
If you don't have an ice cream machine, simply freeze the mixture in a container, then scrape ice into flakes with a fork to make a granita.

A spring picnic

Green is the colour of spring, and this is reflected in the food: there are freshly podded peas, of course, and wild greens. Spring rabbits and the first strawberries of the season are also on the menu.

After being cooped up all winter, the urge to step out into the lush green foliage and slowly warming days for a spring picnic is irresistible.

Chilled pea and coriander soup

Serves 6 as a starter

I read somewhere that peas picked and eaten fresh are reason enough to grow a garden, and I'd second that – they are among mine and my son Tristan's favourite vegetables. This chilled soup has that intense 'green' flavour of peas, sweetness from their natural sugars and toasted spices to round out the experience. A beautiful start to a picnic or just a meal at home.

50 ml olive oil
3 spring onions, thinly sliced
2 teaspoons black mustard seeds
1 teaspoon coriander seeds
1 teaspoon ground fennel
200 g shelled peas (from about 500 g peas in pods)
500 ml (2 cups) chicken or vegetable stock
sea salt and freshly ground black pepper
vegetable oil, for deep-frying
2 golden shallots, thinly sliced
crème fraîche, to serve
large handful coriander leaves

Heat olive oil in a large saucepan over medium heat, add spring onions and sauté until fragrant, about 1 minute. Add spices and continue to cook for 2–3 minutes or until spices are fragrant and mustard seeds begin to pop. Add peas and stock to saucepan and bring to the boil, then immediately remove from the heat and pour into a blender. Allow to cool for a few minutes before puréeing until smooth. Season soup with salt and pepper and refrigerate until required.

For crispy shallots, pour a 3 cm depth of vegetable oil into a small saucepan and heat to 180°C. Add shallots and fry until light golden and crisp. Using a slotted spoon, transfer shallots to a plate lined with paper towel to drain.

Serve soup topped with a spoonful of crème fraîche, some crispy shallots and coriander leaves.

Confit rabbit and pickled vegetable sandwich

Serves 6

Sometimes I think anything cooked slowly in pork fat would taste delicious. Here I have opted for rabbit, but chicken could easily be substituted. The pickled vegetables add the perfect piquancy to balance the confit in a sandwich.

1 × 1.2 kg rabbit, cut into 10 pieces (front and back legs jointed and saddle cut into 6 pieces)
2 tablespoons sea salt
2 bay leaves, torn
2 cloves garlic, thinly sliced
2 kg duck or pork fat
12 small soft bread rolls

pickled vegetables
8 baby carrots, halved lengthways
6 small radishes
300 g lettuce hearts
250 g baby cucumbers
50 g fine sea salt
1 litre (4 cups) white wine vinegar
220 g (1 cup) caster sugar
2 cloves garlic, thinly sliced
1 teaspoon caraway seeds
4 cloves

garlic and anchovy mayonnaise
3 cloves garlic
3 anchovy fillets
30 ml lemon juice
2 egg yolks
200 ml extra virgin olive oil
sea salt and freshly ground black pepper

Place rabbit pieces in a non-metallic ovenproof dish that will hold them snugly. Scatter evenly with salt, bay leaves and garlic, then cover and refrigerate overnight.

Next day remove rabbit from dish, reserving garlic and bay leaves. Rinse rabbit under cold running water, pat dry with paper towel and return to rinsed-out dish with bay leaves and garlic. Preheat oven to 120°C.

Melt fat in a saucepan then pour over rabbit. Cover dish with foil, then place in oven and cook for 3 hours. Remove and set aside to cool. The confit will keep, immersed in fat and refrigerated, for up to 2 weeks; to retrieve individual pieces, use a clean sterilised spoon.

For pickled vegetables, place all vegetables in a non-metallic bowl, scatter over salt and mix to combine. Cover bowl and set aside at room temperature for 2 hours. Meanwhile, combine vinegar, sugar, garlic and spices in a non-reactive saucepan. Stir over medium heat until sugar has dissolved, then set aside to cool to room temperature. Rinse salt from vegetables and pat dry using a clean tea towel. Combine vegetables and pickling liquid and refrigerate for at least 3 hours (they will keep for several weeks in the fridge).

For garlic and anchovy mayonnaise, place garlic, anchovies, lemon juice and egg yolks into the bowl of a food processor and process until smooth, light and frothy. With the motor running, add oil in a thin steady stream until mayonnaise is thick and emulsified, then season with salt and pepper and refrigerate until required.

Halve bread rolls, spread some mayonnaise over each side, then fill with shredded rabbit and drained pickles and serve.

Note

To sterilise a spoon, simply pour boiling water over it. Using a sterilised spoon avoids introducing anything undesirable into the confit.

Smoked trout and fennel tart

Serves 8

The base of this recipe comes from my good friend Alistair Wise, pastry chef extraordinaire. Alistair teaches all of our pastry classes at The Agrarian Kitchen and has been battle-hardened in the kitchens of Gordon Ramsay. This is by far the most balanced and delicious tart I have ever tasted, but the filling must be cooked only until it is just set. I have opted for some smoked fish and shaved fennel on top, but feel free to experiment – try sliced tomato and goat's cheese or jamón with shaved celery and carrots.

1 baby fennel bulb
1 tablespoon lemon juice
250 g smoked trout or salmon

savoury shortcrust pastry
250 g plain flour
125 g cold unsalted butter, chopped
¾ teaspoon fine sea salt
90 ml milk
1 egg, beaten

filling
500 ml cream
200 ml milk
8 eggs
1 teaspoon fine sea salt

For pastry, combine flour, butter and salt in a large bowl. Using your fingertips, rub in butter until the mixture resembles breadcrumbs, then add milk and gently mix to form a dough. Flatten into a disc, wrap in plastic film and refrigerate for at least 1 hour.

On a clean, lightly floured workbench, roll out pastry to 5 mm thick and line a 22 cm round flan tin, gently easing pastry into base and corners. Using a sharp knife, trim excess pastry, then refrigerate pastry shell for 30 minutes.

Preheat oven to 180°C. Line pastry shell with baking paper and fill with pastry weights or dried beans, then blind-bake for 15 minutes. Remove baking paper and pastry weights, then return pastry shell to oven and cook for a further 5–10 minutes or until golden. Brush inside of pastry shell with beaten egg and return to oven for 5 minutes. Remove and reduce oven temperature to 150°C.

For filling, whisk together cream, milk, eggs and salt in a bowl. Pour into pastry shell and bake for 35–40 minutes or until just set.

Using a mandoline, thinly slice fennel and place in a bowl, then toss with lemon juice. Arrange smoked trout or salmon over tart, scatter over fennel and serve.

SPRING ◇ PAGE 49

Potato and wild green salad with anchovy dressing

Serves 6

If you're lucky enough to live close to some good foraging, this salad can be partially prepared at home and the remaining ingredients gathered on the way or at the picnic site. Of course you can use baby spinach, wild rocket and/or mizuna, but it is a fabulous feeling to do a little foraging, always provided you are absolutely sure of what you are picking and are confident it hasn't been sprayed.

300 ml milk
6 cloves garlic, peeled
3 anchovy fillets
2 tablespoons white wine vinegar
120 ml extra virgin olive oil
1 teaspoon dijon mustard
sea salt and freshly ground black pepper
1.2 kg waxy potatoes, such as kipfler or pink fir apple
80 g wild greens (such as chickweed, dandelion and fat hen), washed

For dressing, place milk in a saucepan over medium heat, add garlic cloves and anchovies and bring to a simmer. Cook until garlic is soft, about 10 minutes, then pour contents of pan into a blender. Allow to cool slightly, then add vinegar, olive oil and mustard and blend until smooth. Season with salt and pepper, adjusting acidity with a little extra vinegar if necessary.

Place potatoes in a large saucepan and cover with cold water. Add a pinch of salt and bring to the boil over high heat, then immediately reduce heat to a gentle simmer. Cook until potatoes are tender when pierced with a skewer, about 10–15 minutes. Drain and set aside to cool to room temperature, then slice any larger potatoes in half lengthways.

To serve, place potatoes and wild greens in a large bowl, drizzle with anchovy dressing and toss to combine.

Strawberry and mascarpone rolled sponge

Serves 8

A rolled sponge is not as tricky as it looks: the secret is to roll the sponge as soon as it comes out of the oven. When it cools, it will retain the shape – just be careful, for it will also be more brittle. As there is no baking powder in the sponge mixture, every opportunity needs to be taken to incorporate air, so whisk the eggs and sugar until they are really pale in colour and go gently when folding in the flour.

500 g mascarpone
75 g caster sugar
1 egg, separated
200 g strawberries, hulled and halved

sponge cake
3 eggs
80 g caster sugar
1 teaspoon vanilla extract
80 g plain flour
¼ teaspoon finely grated lemon rind
1 tablespoon melted butter

For sponge cake, preheat oven to 180°C and line a 32 cm × 22 cm baking tray with baking paper. Using an electric mixer, whisk eggs and sugar until thick and pale and doubled in volume. Add vanilla and whisk until just combined. Sift over one-third of the flour and fold in gently, using a large metal spoon. Sift over remaining flour, then add lemon rind and melted butter and gently fold everything together. Transfer sponge mixture to prepared baking tray, spreading it out evenly, and bake until golden, about 8–10 minutes. Carefully turn out onto a clean tea towel and remove baking paper. Roll up sponge in tea towel, starting from one of the long sides, then leave to cool.

Whisk mascarpone, 50 g sugar and the egg yolk until very thick. In a separate bowl and with a clean whisk, whisk egg white until soft peaks form, then gradually add remaining sugar and whisk to a firm peak. Fold egg white mixture through the mascarpone.

Unroll sponge and remove tea towel. Spread mascarpone mixture over the inside and lay strawberries on top. Carefully roll up sponge, then refrigerate until firm.

To serve, use a serrated knife to cut into 2 cm slices.

Raspberry creams

Makes 14

I love a filled biscuit – somehow they have a sense of occasion about them. In our household, we always had the everyday biscuits Mum baked, but for visitors there would be something like a filled biscuit that took a little extra time and looked more special. The components of these biscuits will all last a while, so you can keep the biscuits in an airtight container, and the cream and jam in the fridge, and assemble them as you need them. Although I think it's also nice when the filled biscuits soften slightly after a day or two, as the jam and cream get to know each other.

185 g soft unsalted butter
120 g brown sugar
1 teaspoon vanilla extract
1 egg
260 g (1¾ cups) plain flour
¾ teaspoon baking powder
120 g icing sugar, plus extra for dusting
80 g (¼ cup) raspberry jam

Preheat oven to 180°C and line 1 large or 2 smaller baking trays with baking paper. Using an electric mixer, beat 175 g butter with brown sugar and vanilla until pale and creamy. Add egg and beat to combine, then sift over flour and baking powder and mix to a firm dough. Roll heaped teaspoons of dough into balls and place on prepared baking trays, pressing lightly to flatten. Bake for 15–20 minutes or until lightly browned. Cool on a wire rack.

Meanwhile, using an electric mixer, beat remaining butter, icing sugar and 1 tablespoon water to a smooth cream.

To assemble, spread a little cream over half the biscuits and spread jam over the other half. Sandwich biscuit halves together and leave for 30 minutes to set. Dust with icing sugar before serving.

Note

Filled raspberry creams will keep in an airtight container for up to 3 days. Un-iced biscuits will keep in an airtight container for up to 1 week.

Rhubarb and rose fizz

Makes about 5 litres

Our neighbour Gwen gave me this recipe for rhubarb fizz, but the rose is my touch: the rose petals should be from the most fragrant rose you can find and, of course, free of chemical sprays. The petals and rhubarb are muddled together and left to infuse overnight for maximum flavour. This refreshing drink is always a big hit, and works well as a non-alcoholic champagne. Depending on the rhubarb used, the fizz may have an attractive pale-pink hue.

800 g rhubarb, chopped
2 handfuls unsprayed rose petals
800 g sugar
1 lemon, sliced
125 ml (½ cup) apple cider vinegar

Combine all ingredients with 5 litres water in a large non-reactive pan or stockpot, cover with a clean tea towel or cloth and leave at room temperature for 24 hours.

Strain through a sieve, then bottle. Using clean plastic bottles will ensure there are no unexpected explosions, but I prefer crown-sealed glass bottles for presentation.

Store in a warm room for 5 days, checking each day for signs of fermentation – the length of time this takes will depend on the temperature. Once you can see bubbles in the bottles, transfer them to the fridge to stop the fermentation.

Consume within 2 months. Keep in mind that the excess sugar will continue to ferment slowly, even at low temperatures, and will eventually turn into alcohol.

Elderflower fizz

Makes about 5 litres

One of my favourite things about spring is the appearance of the elderflowers in our garden. The trees there have grown from seed sown by the birds, as they love the elderberries that appear in summer. Elder trees are also common in Australia's cooler cities, particularly Hobart, so keep your eyes peeled for the tell-tale frothy flowerheads. Their fresh scent bears little resemblance to the lingering floral flavour they leave behind in infusions such as this delicate fizz. Often called elderflower champagne for its fine bead and colour, it can happily fill in for the obligatory glass of bubbles on special occasions.

3 heads elderflower
finely grated rind and juice of 1 lemon
400 g sugar
2 tablespoons white wine vinegar

Shake elderflower blossoms to remove any bugs, but do not wash as this will remove some of the natural wild yeasts. Place blossoms in a large bowl, along with lemon rind, lemon juice, sugar and vinegar.

Place 5 litres water in a large non-reactive pan or stockpot and heat until the water is just warm to the touch (about 35°C), then remove from the heat. Add contents of the bowl, stir to dissolve sugar, then cover with a clean tea towel or cloth and leave at room temperature for 24 hours.

Strain through a sieve, then bottle. Using clean plastic bottles will ensure there are no unexpected explosions, but I prefer crown-sealed glass bottles for presentation.

Let sit for about 2 weeks in a cool room. Once you can see bubbles in the bottles, transfer them to the fridge to stop the fermentation. Consume at your leisure.

Note
Keep in mind that the excess sugar will continue to ferment slowly and will eventually turn into alcohol, so it's probably a good idea to use each batch within a couple of months.

Keeping animals

Meat is a significant and enjoyable part of the human diet for many of us. And while it may not be everybody's cup of tea to keep their own animals for meat, we can at least be aware of what we're eating and how humanely the animal was raised. It is worth remembering that cheap meat is often a result of intensive, industrialised processes – effectively, you get what you pay for. Often it is a question of value, and undoubtedly the best value is to buy smaller amounts of higher-quality, more nutritious meat, while incorporating more vegetables, legumes and grains into our diets.

Pigs were always part of the plan at The Agrarian Kitchen. For several years prior to moving here, we'd been making our own charcuterie, so the next step was to begin raising our own. Our first pigs were two Wessex saddleback gilts (young females) from Lee Christmas, who soon became my mentor for all things pig-related. The pigs were initially moved around the property by means of portable electric fencing, and their first job was as pig ploughs – to dig the space that would eventually become our garden. If you're not after a garden bed, simply scatter the freshly tilled earth with pasture seed and move the pigs onto a fresh piece of ground to start the process again.

Apart from the forage, our pigs get sprouted barley and peas, any spare greens or vegetables from the garden and seasonal treats such as windfall fruit and acorns. Remember that most rare-breed pigs were bred to provide plenty of lard for the table as well and will run to fat if overfed – which is all too tempting when you're greeted with squeals of anticipation from a couple of endearing piglets. The aim is to produce pork that has a good spread of firm fat around it and marbling throughout; in my opinion, the best-flavoured meat is the result of longer, slower growth and a varied diet.

Pigs are very intelligent creatures and deserve to be raised with dignity, and given enough space to move freely. If provided with shade and forage, a varied diet and plenty of clean fresh water to drink and to wallow in during summer, they are happy animals with wonderful temperaments.

The majority of our pigs are destined for our 'Whole Hog' class, a nose-to-tail butchery, cooking and eating experience that pays homage to these wonderful creatures.

We came to goats in a round-about way. Thinking it would be nice to produce our own milk, yoghurt, butter and cheese, I initially bought two Jersey cows. However, we soon learnt that we didn't have enough grazing pasture to support them, and so we sent them on to friends with more land. Then an opportunity arose to purchase two British Alpine dairy goats, and I was hooked.

◇◇

Pigs love to dig and will leave no stone unturned, no weed root uneaten as they turn hard ground into soft friable soil.

Being smaller than cows, goats are somewhat easier to handle and milk – and, for their size, they produce more milk than either cows or sheep. When fresh, the milk lacks the strong 'goaty' flavour that many associate with goat's milk and has a clean minerality to it; the stronger flavours come with age, as the fatty acids break down.

Chickens are usually the first choice for farm animals, not least because fresh eggs are so closely associated with farm life. Our laying chickens are Barnevelders, a Dutch breed that found its way to Tasmania with the Dutch immigrants. A large, dual-purpose breed with a wonderful temperament, they are also hardy birds that will commence laying early in winter, making them ideal for Tasmanian conditions.

Geese are the noblest creatures of the poultry family. Confidently goose-stepping their way around the paddocks, they are very easy to keep. If you are lucky enough to find their eggs, they make excellent eating and even better baked goods; however, they are usually well-camouflaged, covered over with foliage and grasses. The first indication will generally be a goose sitting, which is all too little, too late! The goslings hatch very early in spring and grow quickly. They are ready for the Christmas table, but I find them better eating in autumn when they've had time to fatten properly, which also ensures there'll be plenty of fat for your roast potatoes.

The ducks at The Agrarian Kitchen are truly free-range, travelling between a neighbour's dam and the pig-pens, where they forage for spilt grain. I bought some, was given others and they have since crossed with my neighbour's flock to become many . . .

Guinea fowl are bizarre-looking birds whose origins can be traced back to Africa. The merits of their flesh were first discovered by the French, who brought them back to Europe from their African colonies. Guinea fowl make the most incessant noise, which means they are best kept as far away from the house as possible. They like to roam in groups and aren't the smartest birds in the room, so we often find ourselves rescuing strays unable to find their way back to the flock.

One of our roosters makes his presence felt.

Our goats have a way of winning over everyone who crosses their path, and seem to love human contact.

Our geese are a mish-mash of breeds – some white, some grey.

— chapter two —

summer

FISHING . BEACH BARBECUES . PASSATA CHERRIES AND BERRIES . ICED TEA

In our part of Tasmania, the transition from spring to summer is a gradual one, as the days lengthen and the heat increases; by the time of the summer solstice, it is around 10pm before the sun fully sets. For the most part, our summers are hot and dry, so we soon settle into a pattern of constant watering that keeps us from fondly imagined, long and lazy days of ice-cold drinks and swaying hammocks.

Summer is the crescendo of the gardening year, a time of abundance when all the hard work pays dividends and we're spoilt for choice in the kitchen.

Padrón peppers, jamón and grilled tomato toasts

Serves 4

Padrón peppers are originally from Spain, where they are most commonly flash-fried in a really hot pan and served as tapas with a sprinkle of sea salt. Roughly one in ten are super-spicy, making these peppers perfect for a game of Russian roulette. For some reason, they are one of our best-growing chillies, so if you are in the warmer northern states they should be a doddle to grow. If not, they are becoming increasingly popular in farmers' markets or you could substitute with a mild chilli.

8 × 1 cm slices rustic bread
200 ml extra virgin olive oil, plus extra for drizzling
1.2 kg vine-ripened tomatoes, halved
sea salt flakes and freshly ground black pepper
250 g padrón peppers
1 clove garlic, peeled
8 thin slices jamón or prosciutto

Heat a chargrill pan or barbecue grillplate over medium–high heat. Brush both sides of the bread slices with olive oil, place on grill and cook until toasted, then turn and grill the other side. Remove and set aside.

Brush tomato halves with olive oil and season with salt and pepper. Grill until grill-lines appear and tomato flesh begins to soften, about 4–5 minutes each side.

Heat remaining olive oil in a large frying pan over high heat, add padrón peppers and sauté until skin starts to blacken and blister and peppers begin to soften but still retain some crunch (about 1–2 minutes). Season with salt flakes.

To serve, rub garlic clove over grilled bread, lay a slice of jamón or prosciutto over each slice of bread and top with tomato and padrón peppers. Grind over some black pepper and drizzle with olive oil.

Bar cod in hot and sour soup

Serves 4

What you are after for this soup is a meaty, white-fleshed fish, such as bar cod. I won't list any others here, because that is part of the problem with our consumption of seafood – we all go for the same few species, which means they get overfished while other, equally suitable types get overlooked, so I challenge you to ask your local fishmonger. If you buy the whole fish (providing it is not too large) and get it filleted, you will have the bones and head for the stock; otherwise, your fishmonger will probably be happy to part with some. You can use fish bones and heads (just make sure the gills have been removed), but try to avoid using oily fish for this broth – not that they don't make a good broth, just not for this recipe.

250 g bar cod fillet, cut into 2 cm pieces
200 g tomatoes, cut into wedges
120 g okra, cut into 1 cm slices
2 tablespoons fish sauce
2 long red chillies, finely chopped
40 ml lime juice (from about 2 limes)
sea salt and freshly ground white pepper
30 g mixed baby coriander and holy basil leaves, torn

fish stock
1.5 kg fish bones, coarsely chopped
2 stalks celery, coarsely chopped
1 brown onion, quartered
2 bay leaves
1 tablespoon black peppercorns

For fish stock, combine ingredients in a stockpot or large saucepan and add 2 litres water, or more if needed to just cover everything. Bring to the boil over high heat, then reduce heat to a simmer and cook for 40 minutes. Strain stock and allow to cool slightly. (If not using immediately to make this soup, transfer stock to containers and refrigerate for up to 5 days or freeze for up to 3 weeks.)

In a large saucepan, bring 1.6 litres fish stock to the boil. Add tomatoes and okra, then reduce heat to a simmer and cook for 2–3 minutes. Add bar cod, fish sauce and chilli and poach over very low heat until fish is just cooked through. Remove from heat, then stir through lime juice and adjust seasoning with salt and pepper.

Ladle into bowls, scatter with torn herbs and serve immediately. If you have them, some edible flowers make a beautiful garnish too.

Grilled mackerel with barley, eggplant and garlic yoghurt

Serves 4

Mackerel would have to be one of the most underrated fish in Australia. Ironically, most of the catch is ground into food for farmed fish, which end up with nowhere near the incredible flavour and texture of mackerel. Grilled slowly over coals, it offers a wonderful eating experience: the natural oils in the fish mean it stays juicy and succulent, and the flesh absorbs the smokiness from the grill.

200 g (1 cup) pearl barley
sea salt and freshly ground black pepper
6 japanese eggplants (aubergines), halved lengthways
3 roma (plum) tomatoes, halved lengthways
olive oil, for brushing
2 whole mackerel (about 700 g in total)
large handful flat-leaf parsley leaves
handful mint leaves

garlic yoghurt
140 g (½ cup) plain yoghurt
2 teaspoons tahini
2 cloves garlic, finely grated
50 ml extra virgin olive oil
sea salt and freshly ground black pepper

Bring a saucepan of lightly salted water to the boil over high heat. Add barley, reduce heat to a simmer and cook until just tender, about 8–10 minutes. Drain barley and spread over a tray or large plate to cool.

For garlic yoghurt, combine yoghurt, tahini and garlic in a bowl, then whisk in olive oil in a thin, steady stream. Season with salt and pepper.

Preheat a chargrill pan or barbecue grillplate over high heat. Brush eggplant and tomato with olive oil and season with salt. Place vegetables cut-side down on grill and cook for 3–4 minutes, then turn and cook for another 3–4 minutes or until tender. Remove and set aside on a plate covered with foil.

Brush fish with olive oil and season with salt. Make sure grill is very hot – this will prevent fish from sticking – then place fish carefully on grill and leave untouched for 4–5 minutes. Turn and cook for another 4–5 minutes or until fish is just cooked through but remains juicy.

To serve, scatter barley over a plate, season with salt and pepper, then arrange grilled eggplant and tomato on top. Lay fish on plate, drizzle with garlic yoghurt and scatter with herbs.

Goat's curd stuffed capsicum with confit tomatoes

Serves 4

This dish makes a lovely starter or side. Add some prosciutto or preserved tuna in olive oil and wild rocket, and you have a light lunch. The confit tomatoes are a great thing to have in the fridge, if you're up to making extra.

8 small red capsicums (peppers)
olive oil, for drizzling
200 g goat's curd
60 g finely grated parmesan
1 egg yolk
sea salt and freshly ground black pepper
50 g fresh breadcrumbs
2 cloves garlic, finely chopped

confit tomatoes
500 ml (2 cups) extra virgin olive oil
1.2 kg vine-ripened tomatoes (ideally heirloom varieties), cut into halves – or quarters, if large
6 sprigs thyme
3 cloves garlic, peeled

Preheat oven to 220°C. Place whole capsicums on a baking tray and drizzle with a little olive oil, then roast until skin is blackened and puffy, about 15–20 minutes. Remove capsicums from oven and, using tongs, transfer to a plastic bag and seal. When cool enough to handle, cut away stalk and core, then peel off skin.

Combine goat's curd, parmesan and egg yolk in a bowl and beat together with a wooden spoon or electric beaters, adding salt and pepper to taste. Spoon mixture into a piping bag, then pipe into the cavity of the capsicums and set aside.

For confit tomatoes, heat olive oil in a large saucepan to 100°C. Add tomatoes, thyme and garlic and cook gently without bubbling until tomatoes are tender when pierced with a skewer, about 15–20 minutes. Remove from heat and set aside at room temperature.

Reduce oven temperature to 180°C. Place stuffed capsicums on a baking tray and drizzle with olive oil. Return to oven and cook until goat's curd begins to turn golden brown, about 20 minutes.

Meanwhile, combine breadcrumbs with chopped garlic in a small bowl. Drizzle with a little olive oil and season with salt and pepper, then spread out on a baking tray and toast in oven until golden, about 7–8 minutes.

To serve, arrange capsicums and confit tomatoes on a plate, scatter with breadcrumbs and serve.

A fishing trip

Although I am not the greatest fisherman, I love eating seafood – and there is no better place to cook and eat seafood than at the beach, with saltspray in your face and sand between your toes. This also gives you the chance to forage for seaweed and shellfish from the rockpools to add to the bounty. Just make sure the water is clean and your catch is safe and legal.

Living on an island you are never far away from a beach.

Periwinkle, tomato and mitsuba soup

Serves 6

What I'm about to say will probably put most of you off, but periwinkles are actually sea snails . . . Before you turn the page in horror, I can vouch, hand-on-heart, that they are delicious. If you still can't come at them, it's fine to substitute any mollusc – try clams or mussels. Apart from adding chewy, tasty morsels of meat, the molluscs also give up a wonderful briny juice which, like the water in an oyster, is redolent of the sea. One of the fun parts of eating periwinkles is extracting them from their shells: once cooked, the hard little cap that seals the opening will pop open and you can use a skewer to free the meat from the shell with a pull and a gentle twist.

Mitsuba is a member of the parsley family and indeed is often referred to as Japanese parsley. It has a flavour that is similar to celery and parsley combined, so if you don't have any mitsuba handy, substitute with celery and/or flat-leaf parsley leaves.

2 kg tomatoes
2 tablespoons extra virgin olive oil
1 brown onion, finely chopped
3 cloves garlic, thinly sliced
1 kg periwinkles, scrubbed
20 g mitsuba leaves
sea salt and freshly ground black pepper

Bring a large saucepan of water to the boil over high heat. With a sharp paring knife, score a cross in the end of each tomato, then place in boiling water to blanch for 30 seconds. Using a slotted spoon, transfer tomatoes to a large bowl of iced water to cool. Peel off skins and discard, then finely chop tomatoes and place in a large bowl.

Heat olive oil in a large saucepan over low–medium heat, add onion and garlic and sauté slowly until very soft, about 10 minutes. Add tomatoes, increase heat to medium–high and simmer for 5 minutes, then add periwinkles and cook until they are tender, about 20 minutes.

Stir through mitsuba leaves, season with salt and pepper and serve immediately.

Note
It's a wise precaution to purge molluscs such as periwinkles and clams before cooking them. Simply soak them in lightly salted water for at least an hour, to encourage them to spit out any sand and gravel.

Pacific oysters with cucumber, radish and coriander relish

Serves 4–6

It's a personal thing, but I prefer oysters with some type of adornment. I know that many would view this as heresy, preferring the unadorned natural splendour of a freshly opened oyster. Let's face it, though, for a first-timer this can be downright daunting, and a dressing such as this can make all the difference. In the interests of perfection, I highly recommend a mandoline. I don't care how good you are with a knife, this is one kitchen utensil that won't be relegated to the back of the drawer.

1 small cucumber (about 350 g), halved lengthways and seeded
5 radishes
handful coriander leaves
1 tablespoon caster sugar
1 tablespoon fish sauce
1 tablespoon lemon juice
2 cloves garlic, finely grated
2 dozen pacific oysters, shucked

Using a mandoline with the fine tooth comb fitted or a sharp knife, cut cucumber and radish into fine julienne strips. Combine in a bowl with coriander leaves.

In a separate bowl, whisk together sugar, fish sauce, lemon juice and 1 tablespoon water, then stir through garlic. Add cucumber, radish and coriander and gently toss everything together.

Serve oysters topped with relish.

There's no better way to spend a blue-sky day than casting a line and then cooking your catch on the beach.

Mussel, fennel and pickled bean salad

Serves 6

Speed, simplicity and flavour are the cornerstones of this recipe. That said, the pickled beans do need to be made a couple of days in advance – my apologies if you have just opened to this page and want it now! This is a dish to take to the beach, where you can cook your mussels on a little portable gas burner or campfire, mix it with a couple of other ingredients and you're good to go.

2 tablespoons olive oil
1 kg black mussels, scrubbed and debearded
2 baby fennel bulbs
large handful flat-leaf parsley leaves
2 tablespoons extra virgin olive oil

pickled beans
500 g green beans, trimmed
30 g (¼ cup) sea salt flakes
500 ml (2 cups) white wine vinegar
6 cloves garlic, peeled
55 g (¼ cup) caster sugar
2 teaspoons black peppercorns
3 bay leaves

For pickled beans, combine beans and salt in a non-reactive bowl, cover and set aside for 24 hours. Next day, combine remaining ingredients in a saucepan and stir over medium heat until sugar has dissolved. Set aside to cool. Drain beans and rinse under cold running water to remove salt. Combine beans and vinegar and refrigerate for another 24 hours. (The pickled beans will keep in the fridge for up to 2 months.)

Heat olive oil in a large saucepan over high heat, add mussels, cover and cook for 1–2 minutes, checking often and removing mussels as they open. Set mussels aside to cool. Strain liquid through a fine sieve and reserve.

Using a mandoline or sharp knife, thinly slice fennel crossways, reserving a few fronds. Combine fennel slices and fronds with mussels, parsley and pickled beans.

Drizzle with a little reserved mussel cooking liquid and the extra virgin olive oil, then serve immediately.

Note
It's a wise precaution to purge mussels before cooking them. Simply soak them in lightly salted water for at least an hour, to encourage them to spit out any sand and gravel.

Seawater-boiled lobster with seaweed butter

Serves 6 as a starter

Lobster is a real treat, and needs to be cooked carefully – its flesh is so delicate that it can become overcooked, tough and stringy in the blink of an eye. With the following technique, it gently cooks in just-boiled water; all you have to do is set a timer. Seaweed adds a wonderful minerality, and I love the fact that it has grown alongside the lobster. If you're not into gathering your own, it can be purchased dried from health-food and wholefood stores. Boiled kipfler potatoes are a perfect accompaniment.

sea salt
1 × 800 g southern rock lobster
250 g unsalted butter
35 g finely grated ginger
16 g dried seaweed (such as hijiki, wakame, arame, kombu), coarsely chopped
1 tablespoon lemon juice
1 teaspoon soy sauce

Fill a large saucepan or stockpot with seawater or salted water and bring to the boil over high heat. Remove from heat, add lobster, then cover with a lid and set aside for 12 minutes.

Meanwhile, melt butter in a saucepan over medium heat until sizzling. Add ginger and cook until fragrant, about 1–2 minutes, then stir in seaweed, lemon juice and soy sauce.

Using a sharp knife, halve lobster lengthways, then carefully remove meat from shell. Cut each half into three, then return lobster meat to shell. Place on a serving plate and spoon over seaweed butter.

Plank-grilled striped trumpeter with chargrilled capsicum and anchovy

Serves 6

This is the perfect way to cook a piece of fish over a fire, as you can move it closer or further away, depending on the heat. Firstly, make sure your plank is an untreated piece of sturdy hardwood wide enough to accommodate the fish fillet. Make sure the fire has burnt down to embers before you start cooking – this will take a couple of hours – and that the fillet is firmly fastened to the plank with tie-wire. The rest is just observation and basting, to keep the fish moist. I have chosen striped trumpeter, a quintessential Tasmanian fish, but other firm white-fleshed fish such as snapper work just as well. If all goes well, you may even be lucky enough to catch a fish to cook. To make this dish in the comfort of your own home, simply cook the fish fillet on the barbecue or roast it in the oven.

1.5 kg (about 8) red capsicums (peppers)
80 ml (⅓ cup) extra virgin olive oil, plus extra for drizzling
10 anchovy fillets, thinly sliced lengthways
3 spring onions, thinly sliced
small handful basil leaves, coarsely torn
sea salt and freshly ground black pepper
1.3 kg striped trumpeter fillet

Preheat oven to 220°C. Place whole capsicums on a baking tray and drizzle with a little olive oil, then roast in oven until skin is blackened and puffy, about 15–20 minutes. Remove capsicums from oven and, using tongs, transfer to a plastic bag and seal. When cool enough to handle, cut away stalk and core of capsicums, then peel off skin. Cut flesh into 1 cm wide strips. Combine capsicum strips with olive oil, anchovy, spring onion and basil, then season to taste. If possible, set aside for a few hours or overnight.

Lay fish skin-side down on plank and use tie wire to secure it in place. Brush fish with olive oil from the capsicum and anchovy, then season with salt and pepper.

Position plank vertically in front of fire, about 60 cm from the embers, with the thickest part of the fillet at the base. Lean top of plank slightly toward the fire, then bury base of plank firmly in the ground to prevent it toppling (see picture overleaf). As the fish cooks, baste it with oil from the capsicum and anchovy, and reposition plank as necessary to avoid overcooking the fish.

When fish is just cooked through, remove from plank and serve with chargrilled capsicum and anchovy.

Grilled corn with garlic, chilli and lime yoghurt

Serves 6

Corn doesn't say summer, it screams it! I find the simplest methods of serving it are the best. Corn barely needs to be cooked at all, so give it just enough time on the grill to char lightly; the yoghurt sauce brushed over will caramelise on the corn. If you are growing corn late in the season you can also eat the whole cobs green before the centre hardens – try them sliced and sautéed, or grilled as in this recipe.

6 cobs corn
280 g (1 cup) plain yoghurt
finely grated rind of 2 limes
4 cloves garlic, finely grated
1 long red chilli, finely chopped
sea salt and freshly ground black pepper
2 tablespoons olive oil

Preheat a chargrill pan or barbecue grillplate over medium–high heat. Pull back corn husks and remove fine silks.

Combine yoghurt, lime rind, garlic and chilli in a bowl and season with salt and pepper.

Brush corn with olive oil, place on grill pan or barbecue and cook, turning often, for 5–6 minutes. Baste with yoghurt mixture and cook, turning often, until yoghurt begins to caramelise, about 2 minutes.

Serve corn with remaining yoghurt passed separately.

Treacle spice biscuits

Makes about 18

When it comes to biscuits, there are two types of people in life: dunkers and non-dunkers. I'm a non-dunker. I enjoy the texture of biscuits the way they were meant to be, and can't stand the dunking residue of biscuit crumbs left at the bottom of the cup. My wife Séverine, on the other hand, is an avid dunker. For all you dunkers out there, she gives these biscuits two thumbs up. This actually makes me happy, because I was going for a gingernut style, and I have it on good authority that the gingernut is the king of dunking biscuits.

120 g (⅓ cup) treacle
100 g unsalted butter
150 g (1 cup) plain flour
2 tablespoons sugar
3 teaspoons ground ginger
1 teaspoon bicarbonate of soda
1 teaspoon mixed spice
1 teaspoon ground cinnamon

Preheat oven to 220°C and line 1 large or 2 smaller baking trays with baking paper.

Combine treacle and butter in a small saucepan and stir over low heat until butter has melted. Sift remaining ingredients into a large bowl, add treacle mixture and stir to combine.

Roll tablespoons of the dough into balls and space them, out on the prepared baking trays, leaving about 6 cm in between.

Bake for 5 minutes, then remove trays and reduce oven temperature to 180°C. Use a spatula to flatten the biscuits slightly, then return to oven and bake for a further 10 minutes. Remove and cool on a wire rack. The biscuits will keep in an airtight container for up to 1 week.

Roasted pork neck with corn fritters and tomatillo salsa

Serves 6

Also known as the scotch, the neck is one of the tastiest parts of the pig – basically, a marbled lump of muscle that can be slow-cooked to tenderness. This cut of pork doesn't normally get sold with the skin on, so you may need to order it in advance, but you'll be rewarded with some yummy crackling.

Tomatillos are related to tomatoes and originate from Mexico. Their flavour is what gives Mexican salsa its unique taste, and they are even easier to grow than tomatoes. At a pinch you could substitute green tomatoes or even ripe tomatoes for this dish, though needless to say the flavour won't be quite the same. The Mexican herbs in the corn fritters, namely the Mexican hyssop and epazote, are an indulgent inclusion, I know, but seeds can be found from heirloom seed suppliers (see page 265), or they can just be left out.

1.8 kg pork neck, with skin on
1 tablespoon cumin seeds
sea salt and freshly ground black pepper
lime cheeks, to serve

tomatillo salsa
150 g tomatillos, finely diced
½ cucumber, peeled, seeded and finely chopped
juice of 1 lime
2 teaspoons cumin seeds, toasted and coarsely ground
½ red onion, finely diced
small handful finely chopped mint
1 tablespoon green coriander seeds or chopped coriander leaves
pinch of sugar

corn fritters
2 cobs corn
1 long red chilli, finely chopped
1 tablespoon chopped basil
2 tablespoons chopped coriander
2 teaspoons finely chopped epazote (optional)
1 tablespoon finely chopped Mexican hyssop (optional)
1 baby fennel bulb, thinly sliced
75 g (½ cup) plain flour
1 tablespoon baking powder
vegetable oil, for deep-frying

Preheat oven to 230°C. Using a sharp cook's knife or stanley knife, score pork skin crossways at 5 mm intervals. Combine cumin seeds with 1 tablespoon sea salt and rub all over pork. Place in a roasting tin and roast for 1 hour, then reduce oven temperature to 150°C and cook for a further 1½ hours or until very tender.

Meanwhile, combine all tomatillo salsa ingredients in a small bowl and season with salt and pepper.

For corn fritters, remove husk and silks from corn. Cut each cob in half crossways, so they have a stable base. Stand each piece of cob vertically on a chopping board and, using a sharp knife, cut down each side to remove kernels. Place kernels in a bowl and mix in remaining ingredients, then add 50 ml cold water and stir to combine. Heat vegetable oil in a deep-fryer or large deep saucepan to 180°C. Working in batches, add tablespoonfuls of corn mixture and fry until golden, about 2–3 minutes. Lift out cooked fritters using a slotted spoon and drain on paper towel. Repeat until all corn mixture is cooked.

Serve slices of pork with corn fritters, dollops of salsa and lime cheeks.

Plum and rosemary roast shoulder of pork with spring onion and rocket sauce

Serves 6

Give me a roast shoulder over a leg any day! Having done a lot of work, the shoulder is always more flavoursome, with a healthy amount of intra-muscular fat to baste the meat internally as it cooks. I am a little spoiled for amazing pork, but there are more and more ethical producers out there raising beautiful pork from rare breeds, so seek them out at your nearest farmers' market. Any stonefruit would work with the pork – it's such a winning combination – try apricots, cherries or peaches.

1 × 1.9 kg deboned shoulder of pork
olive oil, for drizzling
sea salt and freshly ground black pepper
3 sprigs rosemary
180 g plums (about 4), halved and stones removed
2 kg kipfler or pink fir apple potatoes, scrubbed and halved lengthways if large
150 g spring onions, finely chopped
50 g wild rocket leaves
150 ml extra virgin olive oil

Preheat oven to 250°C. Using a sharp cook's knife or stanley knife, score pork skin at 5 mm intervals, then drizzle with a little olive oil and rub salt into skin. Place pork skin-side down on a work surface. Strip rosemary leaves from stalks into a mortar, add a pinch of sea salt and bruise rosemary leaves with the pestle. Rub rosemary over inside of pork, then place plum halves in a line down the centre and roll up pork to enclose plums, securing it with butcher's twine.

Place pork in a roasting tin and cook in oven for 40 minutes. Reduce oven temperature to 150°C, add potatoes and toss in juices. Cook for 2 hours or until pork is tender. Remove from oven, cover loosely with foil, and leave to rest for 10 minutes.

Meanwhile, whiz spring onion and rocket in a food processor until coarsely chopped. With the motor running, add extra virgin olive oil in a thin steady stream. Season sauce with salt and pepper.

Using a serrated knife, slice pork and serve with potatoes and spoonfuls of spring onion and rocket sauce.

Poached wagyu beef short-rib with coriander and horseradish relish

Serves 8

Please feel free to use any good-quality beef you can find for this simple dish. It's just that in Tasmania we have access to the most amazing wagyu beef from Robbins Island, which I can never resist. This small island off the top of Tasmania is cow heaven, with lots of long green grass to graze, seasoned by salty sea breezes. Brothers John and Keith Hammond and their families raise their cows entirely on grass, so they never see a feedlot. Grass-fed cows are not only healthier animals, but their meat is also better for us, with high levels of omega-3 and omega-6 fatty acids in the marbling. Grain-fed animals may get fatter quicker, but raising them in this way is akin to us being locked in a room and fed chocolate bars – and, in my opinion, their meat never has the same depth of flavour.

2 tablespoons olive oil
8 × 220 g pieces wagyu beef short-rib
2 brown onions, coarsely chopped
2 carrots, coarsely chopped
4 stalks celery, coarsely chopped
1 bulb garlic, halved crossways
3 bay leaves
2 star anise
1 tablespoon fennel seeds
1 tablespoon black peppercorns
sea salt
fish sauce
handful coriander leaves
handful Thai basil leaves

coriander and horseradish relish
2 tablespoons fish sauce
2 tablespoons lemon juice
1 tablespoon sesame oil
1 small golden shallot, very finely grated
7 cm piece horseradish, peeled and finely grated *or* 1 tablespoon bottled horseradish
100 g coriander stems and leaves, finely chopped

Heat olive oil in a large heavy-based saucepan over high heat, add beef and brown on all sides. Remove beef and drain most of the fat from the pan. Add vegetables, bay leaves and spices and sauté until fragrant, about 8 minutes. Return beef to pan, cover with cold water and bring to the boil. Season with salt, then reduce heat to a simmer and cook, covered, until meat falls apart, about 2½–3 hours. Carefully remove beef and set aside, then strain broth and season to taste with fish sauce.

For coriander and horseradish relish, whisk together fish sauce, lemon juice and sesame oil, then stir in shallot, horseradish and coriander and set aside.

Serve poached beef in large bowls with a little of its broth. Scatter with herb leaves and top with a spoonful of relish.

Chargrilled scotch fillet with chimichurri sauce and buttermilk fried onion rings

Serves 4

Chimichurri is a classic Argentinian sauce traditionally served with grilled beef. Let's face it, those Argentinians know their beef, so this is a hard accompaniment to beat, not just with steak but also chicken or pork – it just works well with anything grilled or barbecued. I'm afraid I often go on about this, but real barbecue is cooking over coals and its flavours are unsurpassed, so trade in your old gas barbecue for a real one and start cooking with fire! This recipe comes courtesy of my old boss and friend Andy Harris, who's now the editor of *Jamie Magazine* in London.

4 × 220 g scotch fillet steaks
2 tablespoons olive oil
sea salt

chimichurri sauce
250 ml (1 cup) extra virgin olive oil
125 ml (½ cup) red wine vinegar
1 onion, finely chopped
2 vine-ripened tomatoes, peeled, seeded and finely chopped
1 long green chilli, finely chopped
2 cloves garlic, finely chopped
small handful finely chopped parsley
small handful finely chopped coriander
1 teaspoon dried oregano
1 teaspoon chilli powder
1 teaspoon paprika
½ teaspoon ground cumin
1 bay leaf, crumbled
sea salt and freshly ground black pepper

buttermilk fried onion rings
3 egg yolks
170 g plain flour
½ teaspoon bicarbonate of soda
1½ teaspoons fine sea salt
350 ml buttermilk
vegetable oil, for deep-frying
4 large onions, cut into rings crossways

For chimichurri sauce, whisk oil and vinegar together in a bowl. Add remaining ingredients, season with salt and pepper and mix well. Leave to stand for at least 2 hours before serving. (Chimichurri sauce will keep refrigerated for up to 5 days.)

For buttermilk fried onion rings, combine egg yolks, flour, bicarbonate of soda and salt in a mixing bowl. Beat together with a large spoon, then slowly pour in buttermilk and stir until batter is smooth. Heat vegetable oil in a deep-fryer or a large deep saucepan to 190°C. Working in batches, dip onion rings into batter and deep-fry for 4–5 minutes or until golden brown. Remove and drain on paper towel. Repeat with remaining onion rings.

Preheat a chargrill pan or barbecue grillplate over medium heat. Brush steaks with olive oil and season with salt, then grill, turning often, for 7–8 minutes for medium–rare. Transfer to a warm plate, cover loosely with foil and leave in a warm place to rest for 5 minutes.

Serve steaks with onion rings and spoonfuls of chimichurri sauce.

Roast chicken with sautéed potatoes and green tomato salad

Serves 4

Chicken has taken on a whole new meaning since we started raising our own. They may not look quite the same, but the depth of flavour has to be tasted to be believed. This is a classic roast chicken, which I find is all the better for being slathered with good lard before cooking (see page 156 for information on rendering lard). In a temperate climate there are always tomatoes that don't get to ripen, so I am always on the lookout for recipes that call for green tomatoes; usually we turn them into chutney, but they have a nice tartness that works well with the rich flavours of a roast. I realise they are a little tricky to buy, though, so just substitute some nice vine-ripened tomatoes if you can't find them.

1 × 1.8 kg chicken
300 g lard or unsalted butter
sea salt
1.7 kg medium-sized potatoes, such as king edward, coliban or red rascal

green tomato salad
800 g green tomatoes (about 5)
2 red onions
3 cloves garlic, crushed
sea salt and freshly ground black pepper
80 ml (⅓ cup) apple cider vinegar

Preheat oven to 220°C. Place chicken in a roasting tin and rub all over with 50 g lard or butter and salt. Roast in oven for 30 minutes, then reduce oven temperature to 150°C and cook for another 30 minutes. Check chicken is cooked by piercing thigh with a skewer – the juices should run clear. Remove chicken from oven, cover loosely with foil and leave to rest for 10 minutes.

While chicken is cooking, make the green tomato salad. Using a mandoline or very sharp knife, slice tomatoes and onions crossways as thinly as possible. Place in a large bowl, stir in garlic and season with salt and pepper. Stir through vinegar and set aside at room temperature until chicken is ready.

Place potatoes in a large saucepan, cover with water and add a pinch of salt. Bring to the boil over high heat, then reduce heat until water is gently simmering and cook potatoes until just tender when pierced with a skewer, about 15 minutes.

Drain potatoes and, when cool enough to handle, peel and set aside. Heat remaining lard or butter in a large heavy-based frying pan, add potatoes and sauté, turning often, until golden and crisp. Season with sea salt flakes.

Cut chicken into pieces and serve with sautéed potatoes and green tomato salad.

SUMMER ◇ PAGE 105

Potato cakes with Sally's tomato kasundi

Serves 4 as a snack

This tomato kasundi recipe comes from Sally Wise, who teaches The Agrarian Kitchen's preserving class. Kasundi is basically an Indian tomato chutney, and Sally's version is hard to beat; I am always quietly chuffed when there are one or two jars left over from the class. I happened to have a jar on the shelf when I was testing these potato cakes and decided they went so well together that the recipe just had to be included. Potatoes grow so well in Tasmania that it is nothing to find five or six named varieties (we grow around twenty) in any greengrocer. I grew up in New South Wales with a choice of two . . . brushed or washed!

200 g self-raising flour, plus extra for dusting
¼ teaspoon baking powder
sea salt
vegetable oil, for deep-frying
1.2 kg floury potatoes, such as king edward or kennebec

Sally's tomato kasundi
1½ tablespoons black mustard seeds
375 ml (1½ cups) apple cider vinegar or white vinegar
20 cloves garlic, roughly chopped
2.5 cm piece ginger, roughly chopped
375 ml (1½ cups) olive oil
20 long red chillies, finely chopped (seeds removed, if preferred)
2 kg ripe tomatoes, diced
1½ tablespoons ground turmeric
4 tablespoons cumin seeds
275 g (1¼ cups) sugar
1 tablespoon sea salt

For Sally's tomato kasundi, soak mustard seeds in a little vinegar for 30 minutes–1 hour. Place garlic and ginger in a blender or food processor, along with soaked mustard seeds and remaining vinegar. Blend on high speed until well puréed. Heat olive oil in a large saucepan, add chilli and tomato and sauté gently for a few minutes until they begin to soften, then add garlic and ginger mixture, plus turmeric, cumin seeds, sugar and salt. Simmer for at least 3 hours or until a chutney-like consistency is reached. Pour into bottles while still warm and seal immediately. (Unopened, bottled kasundi will keep for 12 months in the pantry; once opened, store in the fridge and use within 2 months.)

In a large bowl, whisk flour, baking powder and a pinch of salt with 250 ml (1 cup) water until just combined. Heat vegetable oil in a deep-fryer or large saucepan to 180°C. Scrub potatoes and cut lengthways into 5 mm slices. Dust a few potato slices at a time in flour then dip into batter and place carefully into hot oil. Cook for 4–5 minutes or until golden and tender when pierced with a skewer. Remove using a slotted spoon and drain on paper towel. Repeat with remaining potato slices.

Season potato cakes with salt and serve with tomato kasundi.

Making tomato passata

◇◇◇

Makes 15 litres

The word *passata* is derived from the Italian for 'to pass', and refers to the passing of the fruit through a sieve or specially designed food mill.

Italians tend not to do things by halves, and often several extended families will gather in late summer to preserve enough tomatoes as passata to last them the entire year. As a guide, it will take 1 kg of tomatoes to fill each 750 ml bottle. Traditionally passata is bottled in brown beer bottles with crown seals, which can be washed and reused with new bottle caps each time, but clear glass bottles with screw lids (like those used for commercially produced passata) are becoming more popular among the Italian community.

20 kg ripe tomatoes
sea salt
20 basil leaves (optional)

If you are fortunate enough to possess a mincer with a tomato pulper, you are well prepared to tackle hundreds of kilos in a day, since all that's required is to pass the tomatoes through the mincer, season them with salt to taste and then add a basil leaf to each bottle, if you like.

Otherwise, the tomatoes must first be roasted or boiled for about 20 minutes or so, just to soften them before they are passed through a food mill and bottled.

Wash your chosen bottles or jars in hot soapy water and rinse well. Using a funnel, pour passata into bottles and seal with lids or bottle caps. Stand bottles on a rack or a folded tea towel inside a large stockpot and cover with cold water. Bring to the boil and simmer for at least 45 minutes. Allow water to cool for about half an hour, then remove bottles. Check seals to ensure that a vacuum has been formed (the lid should be slightly inverted in the centre) and allow to cool completely.

Sealed bottles of passata can be stored for at least 12 months in a cool, dry place. Once opened, the contents need to be refrigerated and used within 3 days.

Passata is a time-honoured way of preserving the summer's tomato harvest for the leaner months ahead.

Apricot and lavender pie

Serves 8

Speak to anyone who's anyone about apricots and they will tell you that the best variety is Moorpark. Previously apricots had left me a little nonplussed, as I found them dry, mealy and tasteless, so I was amazed when I first tasted one of these apricots that had been tree-ripened and the juice actually dribbled down my chin. I stumbled on the combination of apricot and lavender through a happy accident: we had inherited some lavender bushes in the garden and when I included a few of the dried flowers in a batch of jam, the reaction was so positive that it's now a rare event when I don't marry the two flavours. If you have English lavender bushes, just let the flowers dry on the plant then trim the heads and strip the flowers into an airtight container before storing in your pantry. Otherwise they can be bought from spice suppliers.

1.4 kg apricots, halved and stones removed
165 g (¾ cup) caster sugar
1 tablespoon lemon juice
1 teaspoon dried lavender flowers
1 egg, beaten with 1 tablespoon water
55 g (¼ cup) raw sugar
cream, to serve

shortcrust pastry
630 g plain flour
350 g cold unsalted butter, cut into 2 cm pieces
120 g caster sugar
sea salt
2 egg yolks

For shortcrust pastry, place flour, butter, sugar and a pinch of salt in a large bowl. Using your fingertips, rub in butter until mixture resembles coarse breadcrumbs. Add egg yolks and 2 tablespoons cold water and gently knead until mixture just comes together. Form pastry into a flat disc, wrap in plastic film and refrigerate until chilled, about 1 hour.

For filling, combine apricot halves, sugar, lemon juice and lavender in a large non-reactive saucepan and cook over medium heat, stirring occasionally, until apricots have just softened, about 15 minutes. Remove from heat and leave to cool to room temperature, then chill until required.

Preheat oven to 180°C. On a lightly floured bench, roll out two-thirds of the shortcrust pastry to a thickness of 4–5 mm, then use to line the base and sides of a 2-litre-capacity pie dish. Spoon in apricot filling, then roll out remaining pastry and lay gently over the pie dish. Trim overhanging pastry with a sharp knife, then press edges between your thumb and fingers to seal. Cut a cross in the centre, brush pie with eggwash and scatter with raw sugar.

Bake pie until golden brown, about 40–45 minutes. Serve warm or at room temperature with cream.

Blood plum and blackberry jelly with vanilla cream

Serves 8

As a kid I detested jelly; it probably didn't help that my uncle Wayne used to call it shivery water. As with most things, though, you really should try it in its best form before you pass judgement. The secret, I find, is to use real fruit juice as the base, and to use only enough gelatine to just set the jelly, so it dissolves as soon as it hits your mouth. The colour of this blood plum and blackberry jelly is incredible, particularly when the light bounces off it at the table. This may be served in individual cups if you fear the consequences of attempting to turn the jelly out of a large mould. Our local antique store, The Drill Hall Emporium, has an amazing range of copper, glass and ceramic Victorian jelly moulds, which make a jelly dessert very special indeed. You'll need to start this up to two days in advance.

1.3 kg blood plums, stones removed, coarsely chopped
560 g blackberries
400 g sugar
9 gold-strength gelatine leaves

vanilla cream
500 ml (2 cups) pouring cream
55 g (¼ cup) sugar
1 vanilla bean, halved lengthways

Combine plums, blackberries, sugar and 2 litres water in a large saucepan. Bring to a simmer over medium heat and cook for 30 minutes or until fruit is soft and pulpy. Pour into a muslin-lined sieve set over a large bowl and leave juice to drain through for 3–4 hours or overnight at room temperature.

Place gelatine leaves in a bowl and cover with cold water. Set aside for 5 minutes or until soft. Measure out 1.4 litres of the plum and blackberry juice and warm in a large saucepan over medium heat, but do not let it boil. Remove gelatine leaves, squeezing out any excess liquid, then add to saucepan and stir until dissolved. Pour mixture into a jelly mould or bowl and refrigerate overnight to set.

For vanilla cream, combine cream, sugar and vanilla bean in a small saucepan and bring to a simmer over medium heat. Remove from heat and set aside for 30 minutes to allow vanilla to infuse. Remove vanilla bean and scrape seeds into cream.

To unmould jelly, place mould in a bowl of warm water until edges just begin to dissolve. Quickly invert mould onto a serving plate and serve the jelly with a jug of vanilla cream.

Fried morello cherry pies

Makes 6

One could get seriously addicted to these pies . . . think the best McDonald's apple pie you've ever had. Which leads me to my next thought: try these with whatever fruit you have on hand – apricots, plums, apples, peaches, nectarines, pears, etc. All you need to do is cook your chosen fruit with some sugar into a jam-like consistency first.

Morello cherries are sour cherries, which means they are not good for eating raw; however, they do make wonderful jam and are the best for cooking (if you've ever tried cooking sweet cherries, you will know that they lose much of their flavour in the process). As morellos are hard to get, I've suggested using jam, which you will find in the continental section of most supermarkets. A word of caution before you start: the pastry is incredibly short and crumbly, so needs careful handling; this does, however, mean it melts in the mouth.

400 g morello cherry jam
1 tablespoon cornflour
vegetable oil, for deep-frying
220 g (1 cup) caster sugar
1 tablespoon ground cinnamon
thick cream, to serve

pastry
330 g plain flour
2 teaspoons fine sea salt
2 teaspoons caster sugar
230 g cold unsalted butter, chopped
70 g cold lard, chopped

For pastry, combine flour, salt and sugar in a large bowl. Add butter and lard and rub between your fingertips until mixture resembles fine breadcrumbs. Add 120 ml cold water and stir to combine, then turn out onto a clean work surface and gently knead until smooth. Wrap dough in plastic film and refrigerate for at least 1 hour.

Place jam in a small saucepan over medium–high heat and bring to a simmer. Mix cornflour with 1 tablespoon cold water until smooth, then add to jam and stir over low heat until it thickens. Remove from heat and set aside to cool.

Heat vegetable oil in a deep-fryer or large deep saucepan to 180°C. Combine sugar and cinnamon in a wide shallow bowl. On a lightly floured bench, roll out pastry to a thickness of 5 mm and cut out 6 rounds about 12 cm in diameter. Spoon 2 tablespoons jam into the middle of each round and fold over to enclose. Using a fork, press the edges together to seal.

Working in batches, carefully slip a few pies at a time into the hot oil and cook for 3–4 minutes or until golden. Remove using a slotted spoon and drain on paper towel, then roll in the sugar and cinnamon. Repeat with remaining pies and serve warm with cream.

Raspberry, strawberry and rose meringues

Serves 8

Lachlan, the hamlet in which we now reside, was once famous for its berries; the cold winters and warm summers are exactly what they need to thrive. Today all that's left of this berry-growing heritage are brothers Nigel and Scott Graham. They grow the best organic raspberries, which we buy when our own canes come up a little short.

125 g raspberries
250 g strawberries, thickly sliced
1 tablespoon caster sugar
handful unsprayed rose petals
2 teaspoons rosewater
300 ml pouring cream

meringues
3 egg whites
pinch of fine sea salt
140 g caster sugar

For meringues, preheat oven to 150°C and line 1 large or 2 smaller baking trays with baking paper. Whisk egg whites and salt in an electric mixer until soft peaks form. With motor running, add sugar a little at a time, ensuring each addition has dissolved before adding the next. Place spoonfuls of meringue mixture onto prepared baking trays and bake until crisp, about 20 minutes. Turn off oven, leave door slightly ajar and allow meringues to cool completely before removing.

Meanwhile, combine raspberries, strawberries, sugar, rose petals and rosewater and set aside at room temperature for at least 30 minutes. Whisk cream in a large bowl to soft peaks.

Spoon rose-infused berry mixture into bowls, top with meringues and a spoonful of cream and serve immediately.

Melon with honeydew and lemongrass granita

Serves 4

It's only in the last few years that we have cracked melon-growing in our hothouses, and some of the first melons we ripened were honeydews. Until then, I'd never really had a good one and couldn't work out why anyone even bothered with them. But that view was flipped on its head when I tried our home-grown honeydews. What a revelation! They actually had a flavour, and juice like sweet, sweet honey nectar. Finally, I could see how they got their name.

This dish would work well as a dessert on a balmy summer's night, but my first thought was of breakfast: it needs to be eaten outside, when the heat of the summer sun is already beating down, and the combination of sweet melons and icy granita with creamy yoghurt offers the perfect antidote.

1 honeydew melon (about 850 g)
110 g (½ cup) caster sugar
4 stalks lemongrass, coarsely chopped
1 tablespoon lemon juice
1 rockmelon (about 900 g)
½ small yellow or red watermelon (about 900 g)
200 g greek yoghurt

Halve honeydew melon and peel, then use a large spoon to scrape out seeds. Coarsely chop honeydew flesh and refrigerate until required.

Combine sugar, lemongrass and 125 ml (½ cup) water in a small saucepan and stir over medium heat until sugar has dissolved. Increase heat to high and simmer for 5 minutes, then turn off heat and set aside to cool.

Strain lemongrass-infused syrup and place in a food processor with the honeydew melon. Purée until smooth, then stir through lemon juice. Pour mixture into a shallow container and freeze until solid, about 6 hours or overnight.

Halve rockmelon, peel and remove seeds, the cut into slices. Peel watermelon and cut into slices.

Divide rockmelon and watermelon among serving bowls and drizzle with yoghurt. Using a fork, scrape honeydew granita into flakes and spoon over melons, then serve immediately.

Buttermilk blueberry scones with honey butter

Makes 20

Every country cook worth their salt will have a good scone recipe, one that can be thrown together as the guests are coming up the driveway and be on the table with a pot of tea inside twenty minutes. The buttermilk in the scone dough is a by-product of making the butter – and anybody who has ever over-whipped cream has unwittingly made butter. It is quick and simple, and also makes a great spread for crumpets.

375 ml (1½ cups) cream
120 g honey
300 g (2 cups) self-raising flour
1 teaspoon fine sea salt
50 g unsalted butter
90 g blueberries
milk, for brushing

Whisk cream in an electric mixer until it separates into large yellow clumps of butter and a whey-like liquid. Pour through a sieve set over a bowl and reserve liquid – this is the buttermilk for the scones. Rinse butter under cold water, massaging to remove any traces of buttermilk, as these will cause the butter to turn rancid more quickly.

For honey butter, return butter to cleaned-out bowl of electric mixer, add honey and beat until smooth and well combined.

Preheat oven to 200°C and line a baking tray with baking paper.

Sift or stir flour and salt together, then use your fingertips to rub in unsalted butter until mixture resembles coarse breadcrumbs. Make a well in the centre, pour in 250 ml (1 cup) buttermilk and mix with a knife to a soft dough, then stir in blueberries. Turn out onto a lightly floured bench and knead very lightly – the dough should be soft and slightly sticky. Press out with your hands to a thickness of 4 cm. Using a round cutter about 5 cm in diameter, press out scones and place them touching each other on the prepared baking tray.

Brush tops of scones with milk and bake until golden brown, about 15 minutes. Serve with honey butter.

The beehive

I have always been fascinated by bees – but when I began trying to grow food crops, this rapidly became an obsession, as I soon realised that not much can happen without them. Most fruit, nut and vegetable crops require pollination, and bees are nature's most effective pollinator. In Tasmania we have many species of native bees and introduced European honeybees – as well as bumblebees, which are like B52 bombers in comparison. There are over 20 000 species of bees worldwide, but the one humans have collected honey from for centuries is the European honeybee. Thanks to its abundance of native flora, Tasmania has a thriving honey industry, the most famous being from an unassuming tree called leatherwood.

The Agrarian Kitchen started out with two hives of European honeybees, and we have successfully captured another swarm to take that to three. The hives are located in the far right-hand corner of the property, close to water, in line with the rays of the morning sun and well away from our guests. The bees will travel approximately a three-kilometre radius from the hive, which means many of our neighbours benefit from their pollination services as well. In return, they stock the hives with golden honey.

Bees use the warm weather of spring, summer and autumn to gather food stores for the winter. It just so happens that they are so efficient at this that we are able to harvest some of the honey for our own use. Production varies from year to year, depending on the strength of the hive, weather conditions and the amount of blossom on offer. Throughout the season the bees will move from plant to plant as they flower, resulting in different coloured and flavoured honey. Commercial beekeepers will follow particular flowerings of plant species in order to create the monofloral honeys, such as blue gum, prickly box, leatherwood and so on. Here the beehives stay put, so we would describe our own harvest as bush honey.

When honey is deposited into a cell in the hive, it is left to dry until it reaches precisely the correct sugar level that will prevent fermentation (in its pure state, honey will last forever), and then it is capped with wax. Remarkably, the bees keep the hive at a constant temperature of 35°C all year round. Finally, to put this all in perspective, a single bee in its lifetime will make one teaspoon of honey . . . something to think about when you are spreading it over your toast. Make sure you enjoy every last drop.

When gathering honey, it is extremely important
to leave enough for the bees over winter.

Blood plum spice cake

Serves 8–10

Baking is a regular part of life here at The Agrarian Kitchen, as for each class we make what has been dubbed 'the sweet treat'. This means we're always on the look out for new and interesting cakes, slices and biscuits. Partly this quest is for our guests, of course, but it's also because we treat ourselves to the leftovers with a late night cup of tea, and it's amazing how quickly you get sick of the same thing. This recipe only gets a run from mid- to late summer, when plums are in season; any plums will work well, but the best for colour are blood plums.

2 tablespoons raw sugar
400 g blood plums (about 10), halved and stones removed
225 g soft unsalted butter, plus extra for greasing tin
270 g (¾ cup) golden syrup
3 eggs
225 g (1½ cups) plain flour
2 teaspoons baking powder
2 teaspoons ground ginger
2 teaspoons ground cinnamon
1 teaspoon ground cloves

Preheat oven to 180°C. Brush base and sides of a 20 cm round cake tin with butter, then line the base with baking paper and dust the sides with flour.

Scatter sugar over base of tin and lay plum halves on top, cut-side down, fitting them snugly in a single layer.

Using an electric mixer, cream butter and golden syrup until pale, then add eggs one at a time, beating well between each addition. Sift over flour, baking powder and spices and stir to combine, then spoon over plums.

Bake for 40–45 minutes or until a skewer inserted in the centre comes out clean. Allow to cool slightly in tin, then turn out onto a wire rack and cool completely. The cake will keep for up to 3 days in an airtight container.

Peach and lemon balm ices

Makes about 4–6 ice blocks (1.2 litres liquid)

Peaches are my favourite stonefruit; perhaps it is their fleeting season or the way the juice of a really ripe peach dribbles down your chin. If you have another favourite stonefruit, feel free to use that – just keep the weight of fruit about the same. Lemon balm is a herb that once planted runs rampant, particularly due to its lineage as part of the mint family. Any of the lemon-flavoured herbs, such as lemongrass, lemon verbena or lemon basil, will do the job here. You'll also need 6 ice-block moulds, or you can improvise with paper cups and wooden lolly sticks.

220 g (1 cup) sugar
1 tablespoon lemon juice
small handful lemon balm leaves
1 kg ripe peaches, halved and stones removed

Combine sugar with 250 ml (1 cup) water in a saucepan and stir over medium heat until sugar has dissolved, then increase heat to high and bring to the boil. Remove pan from heat and stir in lemon juice and lemon balm leaves. Cover and set aside for at least 30 minutes.

Coarsely chop peach flesh, then place in a blender with the lemon balm syrup and process until smooth. Pour mixture into ice-block moulds or paper cups and freeze for at least 6 hours or overnight. If using paper cups, allow the mixture to half-freeze, then press a wooden stick into the middle of each one and return to freezer until frozen solid.

Peach, mint and passionfruit iced tea

Makes about 2.5 litres

On a hot summer's day there are few drinks more refreshing than iced tea. Traditionally it is flavoured with a few slices of lemon and/or some sprigs of mint, but the range of flavours now offered commercially illustrates how well fruit and iced tea go together. One of my favourites is peach, so I set out to replicate it at home, with surprisingly good results: the simple act of macerating the peaches and passionfruit in the tea is enough to capture the flavour of the season. As I write this, I'm hoping that those of you with mangoes to spare will try the same experiment.

50 g (½ cup) tea leaves, such as darjeeling
2 teaspoons jasmine tea leaves
160 g caster sugar
360 g peaches (about 2–3), stones removed and flesh cut into thin wedges
190 g passionfruit (about 2–3), pulp scraped into a bowl
sprigs mint
ice, to serve

Pour 1.2 litres water into a large saucepan and bring to the boil over high heat.

Add tea leaves to the boiling water in the saucepan and remove from the heat. Leave tea to steep for 10 minutes, then strain into a large serving jug.

Add sugar and stir until dissolved, then add 800 ml cold water, along with peach slices, passionfruit pulp and mint sprigs. Fill jug with ice and serve.

The garden

Without the garden, there would be no Agrarian Kitchen. The garden grounds us with our part of the world: it is a reflection of the weather and the season in the Lachlan Valley; and, in turn, the meals we prepare and eat are a reflection of the garden. I often get asked by guests what we will be cooking on the day of their class, and the short answer is 'I don't know'. And that, to me, is the most wonderful part of the whole process. From the time the seeds go into the ground, sprout into new life, grow to maturity and are harvested, it is the circle of life – and it can be fickle. Even though I observe the garden every day, I find the changes that happen on a daily basis endlessly fascinating.

Setting up the garden involved fencing off a large area of our back paddock and then sending in the pigs to do their work. It is in a pig's nature to dig, so we simply encouraged them do their thing. In a matter of weeks they had turned the ground over and eaten out the weeds, leaving a lovely tilth that we formed into planting beds. The rest comprised many hours of adding manures, mulch, compost and growing green-manure crops. In the early days, parts of the garden flourished while other parts had barely enough topsoil to bury a worm. Now, under the guidance of our head gardener, Rainer, the entire area is highly productive.

From its initial paddock, the garden has grown, spreading into the paddock next door to incorporate hothouses, and taking over parts of the original flower garden around the school. Our vegetable and herb garden is a celebration of the diversity of edible plant species. It now yields an incredible array of vegetables, herbs, berries and fruit trees: over the past five years we have grown 15 varieties of garlic, over 20 kinds of potato and around 200 varieties of tomato. This is the antithesis of the monoculture of supermarket offerings – and, even then, we are just scratching the surface.

Everything is grown using organic principles, with not a pesticide in sight; every weed is pulled or removed with the sharp blade of a hoe. Wherever possible, seeds are saved for future crops, as this allows them to evolve and adapt to our specific environment. Our plan from the beginning was to grow produce naturally, at its own pace, for maximum flavour, rather than pumping it up with artificial fertilisers for quick gratification. This approach means that our focus is mostly on the soil. By feeding it and encouraging the growth of microorganisms, we are creating a healthy, self-sustaining environment in which plants thrive.

Gardening really is about enjoying the journey, for there is no time when you will ever be truly happy with a garden. Even if you chance upon a moment of perfection, perhaps for a split second, it is fleeting.

What we cook each day at The Agrarian Kitchen
depends entirely on what is at its best in the garden.

Of course there are the exceptional wet years, but for the most part our summers are typically Australian: hot and dry. It is this weather that makes the berries ripen so beautifully and means we can grow outdoor crops of tomatoes and corn with relative ease. Not that this stops us from using our hothouses as an insurance policy against cool nights or the occasional cold snap.

The longer daylight hours and warmth of summer cause the garden to burst at the seams with fecundity, and make preserving a necessary pleasure.

— chapter three —

autumn

—

PUMPKINS . FORAGING
MUSHROOMS . APPLES . QUINCES

◇◇

Autumn is the garden's last hurrah. As the days get noticeably shorter, the crops that have basked in the warmth and long days of summer are quickly ripening the last of their fruit. It is time to consider the growing season that has passed, to take stock of the successes and failures. There is plenty of time for reflection as you stand over the stove, preserving the autumn glut . . . and maybe contemplating what you will grow next year.

Cabbage and buckwheat soup with cheese toasts

Serves 4

This soup is testament to the fact that with a few humble ingredients you can make something memorable. As with all soups, a lot of flavour comes from the quality of the stock. I would implore you to make your own, or at least buy proper stock; I have yet to taste anything from a tetra-pack that comes close to the flavour of a genuine stock. The other thing worth mentioning is to make sure you slowly cook your onions until they are really tender – this will caramelise the sugars, giving your soup a beautiful sweetness.

100 g unsalted butter
80 ml (⅓ cup) olive oil
800 g brown onions, thinly sliced
sea salt and freshly ground black pepper
1.5 litres chicken or vegetable stock
2 tablespoons buckwheat
15 g dried porcini mushrooms
150 g cabbage, thinly sliced
2 slices sourdough bread, halved crossways
200 g raclette, tilsit or gruyère cheese, grated

Heat butter and olive oil in a large saucepan over low–medium heat. Add onion and a pinch of salt and sauté gently for about 15 minutes to allow onions to sweat and caramelise.

Add stock to pan, increase heat and bring to a simmer, then add buckwheat and dried mushrooms. Cook until buckwheat is tender, about 10 minutes. Add cabbage to soup and cook until it just wilts. Adjust seasoning with salt and pepper.

Preheat grill to high. Toast bread pieces on one side. Ladle soup into individual ovenproof bowls, then place a piece of toast in the middle of each bowl of soup, toasted-side down, and scatter with cheese. Place bowls under grill to melt cheese. When cheese is golden and bubbling, serve immediately – warn people that the bowls and soup will be very hot!

Beef carpaccio with caponata

Serves 6

When confronted with the prospect of eating raw meat for the first time, most people turn up their nose. But put those preconceptions aside – it is delicious, providing of course that the meat is of high quality. I have used sirloin for this carpaccio as it holds together when pounded flat, but there are many other cuts you could use, such as topside. The caponata in this dish is more like a relish, with the vegetables cut small, providing sweet and sour highlights.

6 × 100 g pieces beef sirloin, sliced 1 cm thick
sea salt and freshly ground black pepper
extra virgin olive oil, for drizzling
finely grated parmesan, to serve

caponata
300 g eggplant (aubergine), cut into 5 mm dice
sea salt and freshly ground black pepper
100 ml extra virgin olive oil
1 stalk celery, finely diced
1 small red capsicum (pepper), seeds removed and flesh finely diced
1 brown onion, finely chopped
3 cloves garlic, finely chopped
150 ml tomato passata
1 tablespoon red wine vinegar
1 teaspoon sugar
50 g (¼ cup) small salted capers, rinsed under warm water
2 teaspoons currants
1 tablespoon pine nuts, toasted

For caponata, place eggplant in a colander, sprinkle with a little salt and toss to combine. Leave for 30 minutes, then rinse well and pat dry. Heat 2 tablespoons olive oil in a frying pan, add celery and cook over medium heat for 5–7 minutes or until soft, then remove from pan and drain on paper towel. Add capsicum to pan and cook for 5–7 minutes or until soft, then remove from pan and drain on paper towel.

Add remaining olive oil to pan, add eggplant and cook, stirring, for 5 minutes or until soft, then remove from pan and drain on paper towel. Add onion and garlic to pan and cook for 5 minutes or until soft, then stir in tomato passata, celery, capsicum, eggplant, vinegar and sugar and season to taste. Cook, stirring frequently, for 10 minutes, then reduce heat to low and simmer for 15 minutes. Add capers, currants and pine nuts and stir to combine. Taste and adjust seasoning, if required.

Place sirloin slices, one at a time, in a clean plastic bag and, using a meat mallet or rolling pin, flatten until they are about 1–2 mm thick.

Arrange sirloin slices on plates, season with salt and pepper, scatter over caponata and drizzle with extra virgin olive oil. Finely grate a little parmesan over the top, then serve immediately.

Baked eggplant and tomato with hommous

Serves 4 as a snack or side

Eggplants are revered in Tasmania. At The Agrarian Kitchen they are strictly a hothouse crop, and one I tend to show with pride and not a little smugness to our guests. Somehow, I never quite get the desired reaction from our Queensland visitors, who tell me they are akin to weeds up there; they are far more excited about the berries that grow like weeds here. It all comes back to the old adage: you always want what you can't have!

750 g (about 4) eggplants (aubergines), cut into 1 cm thick slices
60 ml (¼ cup) olive oil
5 vine-ripened tomatoes, cut into 1 cm thick slices
sea salt and freshly ground black pepper
2 teaspoons cumin seeds, coarsely ground
flatbread and coriander leaves, to serve

hommous
100 g dried chickpeas, soaked overnight in cold water with a pinch of bicarbonate of soda
sea salt and freshly ground black pepper
juice of 1 lemon
2 garlic cloves, crushed
1½ tablespoons tahini
60 ml (¼ cup) extra virgin olive oil

For hommous, drain chickpeas and rinse under cold water, then place in a saucepan, cover with cold water and bring to the boil. Reduce heat and simmer gently for about 1–1½ hours until chickpeas are very tender. Remove from heat, pour off excess liquid until level with chickpeas, then season with salt and pepper and set aside for about 20 minutes. Drain chickpeas, reserving cooking liquid, and place in a food processor. Blend until smooth, adding just enough reserved cooking liquid to help the blades turn. Add lemon juice, garlic, tahini and olive oil and pulse to combine. Taste and adjust as necessary, adding seasoning or more liquid until the flavour and texture are to your liking.

Heat olive oil in a large frying pan and, working in batches, sauté eggplant until golden, about 3–4 minutes each side. Drain on paper towel.

Preheat oven to 180°C. Arrange eggplant and tomato slices alternately in a large ovenproof dish, then season with salt and pepper and scatter with cumin seeds. Drizzle with olive oil and cook in oven until tomatoes are tender, about 30 minutes.

Serve the baked eggplant and tomato with hommous, flatbread and coriander.

Pumpkin, nettle and pancetta rotolo with hazelnut crumbs

Serves 6–8

Rotolo (pictured over the page) is a real favourite here. Essentially, it's an idea, and that idea is: roll some fillings in a giant sheet of pasta, wrap it in a tea towel and poach it. What I really love is its versatility. Not only can the fillings be varied through the seasons, but it also looks super-impressive and can serve a lot of people easily. Nettles are commonly found growing in high-nitrogen soils, so chook pens and sheep and cattle yards are the first places to start looking. You will need gloves to pick them, but once the leaves are cooked the sting softens and is no longer an issue. If you are lucky enough not to have a nettle problem in your garden, almost any leafy greens can be substituted – the easiest would probably be baby spinach, but in the past I have even used mint leaves. If you don't have a fish kettle or a saucepan wide enough to accommodate the rotolo, you can always bend it gently to fit it in your pan, or simply make two smaller ones.

1.3 kg pumpkin, peeled and cut into 2 cm chunks
2 tablespoons olive oil
sea salt and freshly ground black pepper
50 g unsalted butter
6 cloves garlic, thinly sliced
300 g nettles, leaves picked (about 150 g nettle leaves)
14 slices pancetta or prosciutto

pasta dough
150 g (1 cup) plain flour
1 egg

hazelnut crumbs
80 g hazelnut kernels
75 g fresh coarse breadcrumbs
80 g unsalted butter
50 ml olive oil
sea salt and freshly ground black pepper

For pasta dough, place flour in a large bowl. Make a well in the centre, add egg and ½–1 tablespoon cold water then gradually incorporate flour into eggs, working with a fork and then your hands until dough just comes together. Turn dough out onto a lightly floured work surface and knead until smooth. Wrap in plastic film and set aside to rest at room temperature for at least 1 hour (the dough can be refrigerated for up to 24 hours at this point – just bring it back to room temperature before rolling).

Meanwhile, preheat oven to 180°C. Place pumpkin in a roasting tin, drizzle with olive oil, season with salt and pepper and mix to combine. Cook in oven until pumpkin is tender, about 40 minutes, then remove and set aside to cool.

Heat butter in a large frying pan, add garlic and nettle leaves and sauté until leaves have wilted (the heat will also disable their sting). Season to taste and set aside.

Divide pasta dough into two and work with one piece at a time, keeping the other piece covered. Using a pasta machine with rollers set at their widest setting, feed dough through rollers. Fold dough in half lengthways, then feed through rollers again and continue until dough is smooth and silky. Now keep rolling the dough, reducing the setting each time, until pasta sheets are translucent and 1 mm thick.

On a lightly floured workbench, lay pasta sheets side-by-side and trim ends square, so they are about 35 cm long and 15 cm wide. Brush long edges with water and overlap slightly, then press to join and form a single sheet of pasta (still 35 cm long but now about 28 cm wide). Transfer pasta sheet to a clean tea towel, scatter over pumpkin and press lightly to squash. Next add the wilted nettle leaves, spreading them out evenly, and finally the pancetta slices. Starting at one of the long sides, lift the edge of the tea towel and use it to help you firmly roll the pasta, enclosing the filling. Keeping the tea towel wrapped around the rotolo, secure both ends with string, then tie at 5 cm intervals along its length to help rotolo hold its shape during cooking.

To cook the rotolo, fill a fish kettle or large wide saucepan with salted water and bring to the boil. Ease the tea-towel-wrapped rotolo into the boiling water and simmer for 20 minutes.

Meanwhile, for hazelnut crumbs, preheat oven to 180°C. Spread hazelnuts on a baking tray and roast until golden, about 7 minutes, then tip onto a clean tea towel, enclose and rub vigorously to remove skins. Coarsely chop hazelnuts and set aside. Combine breadcrumbs, butter and oil in a bowl and season with salt and pepper. Spread crumbs over a baking tray and roast in oven until golden brown, about 8–10 minutes. Stir through hazelnuts.

Using tongs, carefully remove rotolo from pan and leave to stand on a large oval plate for 5 minutes.

To serve, gently unwrap rotolo and trim ends, then cut into 5 cm slices using a sharp knife. Place slices on plates, scatter with hazelnut crumbs and serve immediately.

Potato, mushroom and pork crackling pizza

Serves 4

With a magnificent wood-fired oven at our disposal, we have pizza quite often. This rendition, topped with sour cream and pork crackling, was inspired by our German gardener. We always have pork skin left over after making sausages – which means so will your local butcher, and they'll likely be glad to get rid of it. Once fried, any extra can be used to add crunch and richness to all sorts of dishes, from salads to soups. The beautifully meaty mushrooms on the pizza in the photo are wild birch boletes, but field mushrooms will be fine.

300 g pork skin, cut into 5 mm dice
120 g (½ cup) sour cream
2 potatoes (about 400 g), cut into 1–2 mm slices
2 large mushrooms, cut into 1 cm slices
1 tablespoon thyme leaves
2 tablespoons extra virgin olive oil

pizza dough
1 tablespoon dried yeast
500 g bread flour
1 teaspoon sea salt

For pizza dough, place dried yeast in a small bowl and stir in just enough water (about 3 tablespoons) to make a smooth paste. In a large bowl, combine flour and salt, then add yeast mixture and 300 ml lukewarm water. Using your hands, mix to a rough dough, then turn dough out onto bench and knead until smooth and elastic – this will take about 10 minutes. Return dough to bowl, cover with a tea towel and set aside in a warm spot to prove.

Meanwhile, make pork crackling. Place pork skin in a frying pan and stir over medium–high heat until fat begins to render and skin begins to sizzle. Cook, stirring constantly, until skin is crisp, about 7–8 minutes. Remove crackling with a slotted spoon and drain on paper towel.

When dough has doubled in size, about 1–2 hours, knock back dough by pressing to deflate and kneading briefly. Divide dough into four, place on a lightly floured workbench and cover loosely with a clean tea towel.

Preheat oven to 250°C, with a pizza stone placed in the centre of the oven.

When dough has again doubled in size, about 30 minutes, lightly flour the base of an upturned baking tray and place a piece of dough on it. With your fingertips, press out the dough until it is about 5 mm thick. Using a spoon, smear a quarter of the sour cream over the dough, then top with a quarter of the potato and mushroom. Scatter with thyme and pork skin and drizzle with a little olive oil. Carefully slide onto the hot pizza stone in the oven and cook until golden, about 10 minutes. Repeat with remaining dough and ingredients.

Serve the pizzas straight from the oven.

Note
Pizza stones can be purchased from kitchenware shops, and will give your pizza a good crisp crust.

Potato gnocchi with braised goat

Serves 6

The secret to good gnocchi lies in the texture of the dough: it should be tacky, not sticky, when you touch it with the palm of your hand. Good gnocchi should be light to eat, so don't over-knead the dough. If you wish to go the extra step and shape the gnocchi, find an old butter pat or ask at your nearest kitchenware store for a gnocchi board. Traditionally, gnocchi are rolled over the tines of a fork, but a board is much easier. Goat meat is wonderful to cook with and can often be found at Italian and Middle Eastern butchers, or you can substitute lamb.

60 ml (¼ cup) olive oil
800 g goat shoulder meat, cut into 5 cm pieces
1 brown onion, finely chopped
4 cloves garlic, thinly sliced
sea salt
1 baby fennel bulb, thinly sliced crossways
2 tablespoons tomato paste (purée)
300 ml chicken stock
60 g green olives, pitted and coarsely chopped
1 tablespoon small salted capers, rinsed
¼ preserved lemon, rind only, thinly sliced
freshly grated parmesan, to serve

potato gnocchi
1 kg desiree potatoes
2 eggs, lightly beaten
250 g plain flour
120 g finely grated parmesan
pinch of nutmeg
sea salt and freshly ground black pepper

Preheat oven to 150°C. Heat olive oil in a large flameproof casserole with a lid over high heat, add goat and brown on all sides, then transfer to a plate. Reduce heat to low–medium, add onion and garlic, plus a pinch of salt, and sauté, stirring occasionally, until onion is very tender, about 10 minutes. Add fennel and cook until beginning to wilt. Return goat to casserole, add tomato paste, increase heat to medium and cook for 2–3 minutes. Add stock and bring to a simmer, then cover casserole with lid and cook in oven for 3 hours or until goat is very tender.

For gnocchi, place unpeeled potatoes in a large saucepan of cold salted water, bring to the boil and cook until tender, about 15–20 minutes. Drain and leave to cool slightly, then peel and pass through a potato ricer or mash until smooth. Combine potato, egg, flour, parmesan and nutmeg in a large bowl and gently mix until just combined. Season to taste with salt and pepper, mixing it in well. Bring a large saucepan of lightly salted water to the boil over high heat.

On a lightly floured work surface, use your hands to roll portions of the dough into logs about 1.5 cm wide, then cut into 2.5 cm pieces. Working in batches, cook gnocchi in the boiling water until they float to the surface. Using a slotted spoon, transfer to a lightly oiled tray or large plate. Repeat with remaining dough.

Shred goat meat using two forks, then add olives, capers and preserved lemon to the casserole and bring to a simmer over medium heat. Add gnocchi and stir to combine. Season to taste with salt and pepper, then serve scattered with freshly grated parmesan.

Guinea fowl cooked in clay with crisp cavolo nero and barley salad

Serves 4

Apart from the impressive display when the clay is smashed open at the table to reveal the bird, the other reason for cooking this way is that it keeps the flesh beautifully moist and allows the flavours to permeate right through. Any bird can be cooked this way, but guinea fowl has very little fat of its own to keep it moist and is particularly delicious – the saving grace for an otherwise dim-witted and noisy bird! White clay is available at craft shops or from online pottery suppliers.

1 guinea fowl (about 950 g)
2 tablespoons olive oil
sea salt and freshly ground black pepper
1 bunch marjoram
1 lemon, quartered, plus extra to serve (optional)
1.5 kg white clay

crisp cavolo nero and barley salad
200 g (1 cup) pearl barley
300 ml olive oil
150 g cavolo nero, finely shredded
250 g mushrooms (ideally shiitake, pine or slippery jack), sliced
2 tablespoons lemon juice
sea salt and freshly ground black pepper

Preheat oven to 190°C. Rub guinea fowl all over with olive oil and season with salt and pepper. Insert marjoram and lemon into cavity. Roll out clay on a lightly floured work surface until it is large enough to wrap guinea fowl. Put guinea fowl in the centre and fold clay over to enclose completely, pressing the edges together to seal. Place on a baking tray and cook in oven for 60 minutes.

Meanwhile, make the crisp cavolo nero and barley salad. Bring a saucepan of lightly salted water to the boil. Add barley and cook until tender, about 12 minutes, then drain and tip into a bowl. Heat olive oil in a wide deep saucepan, then add cavolo nero and sauté until crisp, about 3–4 minutes. Using a slotted spoon, transfer cavolo nero to a plate lined with paper towel to drain. Spoon a little of the oil from the saucepan into a frying pan, add mushrooms and sauté over medium–high heat until tender. Add cavolo nero and mushrooms to bowl of barley and mix well. Drizzle with lemon juice and extra oil, if needed, and season to taste.

Remove guinea fowl from oven and set aside to rest for 10 minutes. Break open clay – a whack from the back of a hefty knife should do it, or use a meat mallet if you have one. Carve guinea fowl into portions, then serve with crisp cavolo nero and barley salad and extra lemon if required.

Fried rabbit with chilli, garlic and spring onion

Serves 6

A lot of the flavour in this dish comes down to the quality of the lard, as well as the rabbit, of course. If you can find freshly rendered lard from a butcher, I highly recommend using it – or go the whole hog and do it yourself at home (see page 156). Start this recipe a day ahead.

1 rabbit, cut into 10 pieces (front and back legs jointed and saddle cut into 6 pieces)
600 ml buttermilk
500 g good-quality lard
250 g unsalted butter
300 g (2 cups) plain flour
50 g (⅓ cup) cornflour
2 teaspoons sea salt
1 teaspoon freshly ground black pepper
1 long red chilli, finely chopped
2 garlic cloves, finely chopped
3 spring onions, finely chopped

Place rabbit in a non-reactive container, pour over buttermilk and refrigerate for 8 hours or overnight. Remove rabbit from buttermilk and place on a wire rack to drain.

In a large saucepan or deep frying pan, combine lard and butter and melt over low heat, skimming foam from surface, for about 5 minutes or until butter stops foaming. Increase heat to high and continue heating the fat until it reaches 180°C.

In a bowl, mix both flours with the salt and pepper. Working in batches, dust rabbit pieces in seasoned flour, shaking off any excess, then fry, skin-side down, for 5–6 minutes. Turn and cook for another 5–6 minutes until golden brown and cooked through, then drain on paper towel. Repeat with remaining rabbit.

Combine chilli, garlic and spring onions, scatter over rabbit and serve immediately.

Rendering lard

The mere mention of cooking with lard is enough to make most people run a mile. This reaction, however, is largely due to the misinformation spread about lard in recent times. Lard has been maligned as an unadulterated, artery-clogging saturated fat consumed by our forebears who lacked our wisdom and access to low-cholesterol oil-based spreads. In actual fact, lard has less saturated fat than butter, contains no trans-fats and is one of nature's best sources of vitamin D. The once-championed margarine spreads, on the other hand, have now been found to be worse for our bodies than the lard and butter they were designed to replace. The main problem is that to create margarine, hydrogen is forced through oil, which produces a new type of fatty acid known as trans-fats. Once inside our bodies, these work to create bad cholesterol; there is also evidence to suggest that trans-fats accumulate in the body because the digestive system doesn't know what to do with them.

The best lard is the home-rendered variety, as commercially produced lard is hydrogenated for longer shelf-life. Ask your butcher for pork back fat. To render, cut it into 1 cm pieces and place in a saucepan with about 3 cm water. Simmer over medium–high heat until all the fat has rendered – this will take 1–2 hours – and only crisp, golden cubes remain. These scratchings can also be consumed as a salty snack, but are not for the faint-hearted!

Strain the liquid, which should be clear, through a fine sieve into a clean container. Store lard in an airtight plastic container in the refrigerator until required – it will keep for several months.

The chilled lard will be a pure white colour and can be used for everything from making pastry to frying potatoes, or even just spread on toast.

Once all the fat has rendered, you'll be left
with crisp, golden cubes and a clear liquid that will
solidify into lard as it cools.

Soft tacos with shredded brisket and tomatillos

Serves 6

Since we realised we could make tortillas with wheat flour and our own rendered lard (see page 156), we've never looked back. They are super-easy to make, and have become a regular part of our 'Whole Hog' class, filled with shredded pork shoulder. The beef brisket used here also makes a wonderful filling – I love the way it shreds into neat strands.

A staple of Mexican food, tomatillos are a close relative of the tomato and are really easy to grow; if anything, you'll need to be vigilant to ensure they don't become weeds. We pickle our home-grown tomatillos to serve with this, but canned tomatillos in brine can be used instead. These are available from select delicatessens and Mexican food stores, where you'll also find dried chipotle chillies.

2 tablespoons vegetable oil or lard
1 brown onion, finely chopped
3 cloves garlic, finely chopped
1.5 kg beef brisket, cut into 3 cm pieces
2 teaspoons cumin seeds
1 teaspoon fennel seeds
2 dried chipotle chillies, crumbled
500 ml (2 cups) tomato passata
sea salt and freshly ground black pepper
2 long red chillies, thinly sliced
chopped coriander, to serve
pickled tomatillos, to serve (optional)

wheat flour tortillas
450 g plain flour
120 g cold lard, chopped

Heat oil or lard in a heavy-based saucepan with a lid, add onion and garlic and sauté over low heat until beginning to soften, about 5 minutes. Increase heat to medium–high, add beef and cook, turning occasionally, until browned. Add spices and stir until fragrant, then add tomato passata and bring to a simmer. Cover and allow to gently simmer until meat easily falls apart, about 3 hours.

Meanwhile, to make tortillas, place flour in a large bowl. Add lard and, using your fingertips, rub in until mixture resembles coarse breadcrumbs. Stir 1 teaspoon salt into 250 ml (1 cup) cold water. Make a well in the centre of flour, then pour in the salted water and mix until combined. On a lightly floured surface, knead dough until smooth and elastic. Wrap dough in plastic film and set aside at room temperature for 30 minutes.

Remove beef from pan and, using two forks, coarsely shred the meat, then return to sauce. Season to taste with salt and pepper and place over low heat to keep warm.

Heat a flat griddle or large heavy-based frying pan over low heat. Roll a tablespoon of dough into a circle about 15 cm in diameter, then place on griddle plate or in pan and cook for 1–2 minutes each side, or until just coloured. Repeat with remaining dough, covering the cooked tortillas with a clean tea towel to keep them warm and soft.

Spoon shredded beef into tortillas and serve scattered with chilli, coriander and tomatillos, if using.

Slow-cooked duck with beetroot and mustard leaves

Serves 4

A lot of people seem to get needlessly worked up when it comes to cooking duck. Relax . . . I think it's actually easier to deal with than chicken, as its natural fat content means you don't need to worry about it drying out. This recipe is set-and-forget – well, for 5 hours or so – during which time the fat slowly renders, basting the meat and keeping it succulent and juicy. In contrast, the beetroot is sweet and earthy and the mustard leaves add a sharp pepperiness. Mustard leaves are best grown in spring and autumn, as they don't enjoy summer's heat; a member of the brassica family, they are as simple to grow as lettuce and much more interesting to eat.

1 × 1.8 kg duck
2 tablespoons olive oil
sea salt and freshly ground black pepper
1.2 kg beetroot (about 5)
400 g mustard leaves
100 g walnuts, coarsely chopped

garlic salad cream
4 cloves garlic, peeled
1 teaspoon english mustard
1 tablespoon white wine vinegar
2 tablespoons extra virgin olive oil
1 tablespoon walnut oil

Preheat oven to 120°C. Place duck in a roasting tin and, using a skewer, pierce skin over breast. Drizzle duck with 1 tablespoon olive oil and rub all over, then sprinkle with salt and pepper. Place duck in oven and roast for 5 hours.

Meanwhile, place beetroot in a pan of salted water and bring to the boil. Simmer for about 40 minutes or until tender when pierced with a skewer. Drain and, when cool enough to handle, peel beetroot and cut into wedges.

For garlic salad cream, place garlic and a pinch of salt in a mortar and crush to a smooth paste with the pestle. Add mustard and vinegar and whisk until combined, then slowly whisk in oils to emulsify and season to taste.

Heat remaining olive oil in a frying pan, add walnuts and sauté over medium heat until toasted, then drain on paper towel.

Coarsely shred the duck meat using your fingers, then combine with beetroot and mustard leaves. Drizzle with garlic salad cream and scatter with walnuts, then serve.

Polpettone

Serves 8–10

I didn't grow up with meatloaf. The closest I got was seeing children on American sitcoms complaining about it. They had obviously never met its Italian cousin polpettone: a wonderful combination of pork and beef, spices and herbs braised in tomato, porcini mushrooms and red wine to produce a decadent sauce. The recipe feeds an army but makes great leftovers, particularly sandwiched in ciabatta bread.

1.5 kg beef chuck, minced
500 g pork belly, minced
2 stalks celery, finely chopped
1 carrot, finely chopped
1 onion, finely chopped
1 teaspoon ground allspice
½ teaspoon chilli flakes
½ teaspoon ground cinnamon
1 teaspoon fennel seeds
½ teaspoon ground cloves
1 teaspoon chopped rosemary
30 g pancetta, finely chopped
2 teaspoons thyme leaves
½ teaspoon chopped marjoram
finely grated rind of 1 lemon
1 egg, lightly beaten
sea salt and freshly ground black pepper
1 × 800 g can whole peeled tomatoes
20 g dried porcini, soaked in 300 ml hot water for 10 minutes
250 ml (1 cup) red wine

Preheat oven to 180°C.

In a large bowl, combine all ingredients except tomatoes, porcini and red wine. Using your hands, mix everything together thoroughly. Roughly shape mixture into a loaf and place in a baking dish.

In another bowl, coarsely crush tomatoes with your hands and combine with porcini and their soaking water and the red wine. Pour this sauce over the meat. Bake, basting occasionally with the sauce, for 1 hour.

Using a serrated knife, slice polpettone and serve with a crisp green salad and crusty bread, or sandwich between two slices of bread.

Venison pie with horseradish

Serves 8

Come hunting season a deer will invariably end up hanging in our cool room. Its dark rich meat is wonderful in so many ways, but braised as a pie filling it is transcendent. The rough puff pastry is a Maggie Beer recipe that has become our first choice for pies. The results are stunning – light and flaky – but if you have a favourite shortcrust recipe, feel free to use that instead.

2 tablespoon olive oil
1.5 kg venison leg meat, cut into 2 cm pieces
2 brown onions, thinly sliced
4 cloves garlic, peeled and thinly sliced
1 long red chilli, thinly sliced
50 g (⅓ cup) plain flour
1 tablespoon freshly ground black pepper
1 tablespoon coriander seeds
2 teaspoons fennel seeds
2 cinnamon sticks
2 bay leaves
450 ml red wine
450 ml beef stock
sea salt
1 egg
125 ml (½ cup) milk
freshly grated horseradish, to serve

rough puff pastry
450 g (3 cups) plain flour
fine sea salt
450 g cold unsalted butter, coarsely grated

Heat olive oil in a heavy-based saucepan over high heat, add venison and cook, turning occasionally, until browned. Transfer meat to a plate. Reduce heat to low, add onion and sauté until very soft, about 10 minutes. Stir through garlic and chilli and return venison to pan. Sprinkle flour over meat, increase heat to medium and cook, stirring occasionally, for 3–4 minutes. Add spices and bay leaves and mix to combine, then add red wine and stock. Bring to a boil, then reduce heat until mixture is just simmering. Cover and cook, stirring occasionally, until meat is tender, about 3 hours. Remove and discard cinnamon sticks and bay leaves. Season to taste with salt. Allow pie filling to cool a little at room temperature, then refrigerate until cold.

For rough puff pastry, sift flour and a pinch of salt onto a work surface, then scatter butter over flour. Using a pastry scraper, cut until roughly mixed. Make a well in the centre, add 180 ml (¾ cup) ice-cold water and mix with the pastry scraper until a dough forms. Divide pastry in half, wrap with plastic film and refrigerate for 20 minutes. Working with one half at a time, roll out on a lightly floured surface to form a rectangle about 1.5 cm thick. Fold the two shorter sides over to meet in the centre, then fold in half again. Cover with plastic film again and refrigerate for 20 minutes to rest. Roll and fold the other half of the pastry, then repeat the rolling, folding and resting process twice more for each half.

On a lightly floured work surface, roll out one half of the pastry into a circle approximately 35 cm in diameter and 5 mm thick, then use to line the base and sides of a deep 20 cm round cake tin. Spoon in the venison filling. Roll out remaining pastry to 5 mm thick and cut out a lid 20 cm in diameter. Place over pie and pinch edges to seal. Whisk together egg and milk and brush over top of pie. Place pie in refrigerator for 20 minutes, to prevent the pastry from shrinking as it cooks.

Meanwhile, preheat oven to 190°C. Bake pie for 50–60 minutes or until golden brown. Serve scattered with freshly grated horseradish.

Foraging for mushrooms

Although some may think of foraging as just another passing food fad, it actually goes much deeper than that – all the crops we grow today have been cultivated from a wild ancestor. For instance all brassicas (cabbages, cauliflowers, broccoli, etc) stem from a single wild cabbage species that is native to the British coastline. In the process of cultivation we may have lost some of the nutritional value of wild plants, but this is made up for by the ease of gathering from a convenient location (your garden, preferably) without any great expenditure of energy.

However, many of us are instinctively drawn to foraging. Luckily for the adventurous, there are still plenty of wild foods for the keen-eyed to forage, even in urban areas. Where we live, we have elderflowers, watercress, chickweed, bulrushes, sheep sorrel, fat hen and nettles in spring; in summer, the elderflowers turn to elderberries, the blackberries burst forth on tangled bushes and the wild apples begin to ripen along the roadsides. Autumn is arguably the best foraging season, as it heralds the arrival of the mushrooms.

When foraging mushrooms, the rule is: if you have the slightest doubt, throw it out. While a good identification manual makes mushrooming easier and safer, you should never eat anything you can't positively identify. Eating the wrong mushroom could kill you, or at the very least leave you with severe gastrointestinal pain. One of the best ways to start is to go with a friend who regularly mushrooms and learn to identify from them.

A good starting point is the humble field mushroom (*Agaricus campestris*): although similar to its cultivated cousin (*Agaricus bisporus*), its flavour is much better. In nearby paddocks you may also find shaggy inkcaps and parasols. Once your curiosity is piqued, the next step is to find the nearest pine forest, where you can seek out slippery jacks and saffron milk caps. When you start foraging, it's amazing what you find: I have discovered wood blewits growing in our next-door neighbour's lawn and birch boletes beneath a row of silver birches along our back fence line.

The best way to preserve your foraged mushrooms is to dry them: slice any larger ones, then dry the mushrooms in a dehydrator or on a rack set over a baking tray in a really low oven (about 60°C) for 5–6 hours or until thoroughly dried. Stored in airtight containers in the pantry, dried mushrooms will keep well for up to a year, ready for that winter braise.

The pleasure we gain from foraging seems
to be hardwired into human beings.

Remember when foraging that it is good etiquette to use a woven basket, so the spores will be spread from the gathered mushrooms as you walk. This ensures more mushrooms in future – not just for your next foraging expedition, but for other foragers as well.

A good mushroom harvest depends on good autumn rainfall, so in some years you'll find your prized mushroom spot deserted, and in other years there'll be mushrooms sprouting everywhere.

Autumn vegetable salad with honey and mustard cream dressing

Serves 4 as a starter or side

Much fuss is made over summer vegetables – think tomatoes, eggplants and zucchini – however, the praises of the humble vegetables of autumn and the cooler months go largely unsung. As the days get shorter and the nights cooler, these vegetables get sweeter. Home-grown brussels sprouts are a revelation, especially if picked when they are small and tender. Disdain for the poor sprout is often the result of a childhood of overcooked, sulphurous, soggy sprouts fit only for the chooks. Be brave: try them again from your own garden or local farmers' market and enjoy!

1.2 kg jerusalem artichokes, scrubbed
800 g baby carrots, scrubbed
1 bulb garlic, cloves separated
50 ml olive oil
sea salt and freshly ground black pepper
300 g tiny brussels sprouts

honey and mustard cream dressing
1 egg yolk
1 tablespoon seeded mustard
1 tablespoon honey
1 tablespoon white wine vinegar
150 ml extra virgin olive oil
50 ml cream
sea salt and freshly ground black pepper

Preheat oven to 200°C. Cut artichokes into halves or quarters if large, then place in a roasting tin. Add carrots and garlic cloves, then drizzle with olive oil and season with salt and pepper. Toss gently to coat all vegetables, then roast until vegetables are tender, about 1 hour and 10 minutes.

For honey and mustard cream dressing, place egg yolk, mustard, honey and vinegar in a small bowl and whisk until pale and frothy, then slowly whisk in olive oil to emulsify. Whisk in cream and season to taste with salt and pepper.

Bring a large saucepan of salted water to the boil, add sprouts and simmer for 1–2 minutes, then drain. Add sprouts to roasted vegetables and toss well to coat in juices. Drizzle with dressing and serve.

Potato latkes with pan-fried apples and coppa

Serves 4

All that's needed here is an initial burst of speed to prevent the grated potato from browning, and then pressing the latke firmly into the pan so the potato's natural starch helps it stick together. As these crisp morsels are the hash brown par excellence, it stands to reason that they also make a nice start to the day – try them with the baked beans on page 230, or a poached egg and some bacon.

1.2 kg floury potatoes, such as kennebec or king edwards
sea salt and freshly ground black pepper
about 125 ml (½ cup) clarified butter (see page 20) or ghee
2 golden delicious apples, cored and cut into wedges
8 slices coppa or prosciutto
120 g (½ cup) crème fraîche or sour cream

Preheat oven to 100°C.

Peel potatoes and coarsely grate into a large bowl. Have another clean bowl ready. Working quickly, take a handful of potato and squeeze firmly to extract as much liquid as possible, then transfer to the second bowl. Repeat until all potato is dry, then season with salt and pepper, mixing well.

Heat 2 tablespoons clarified butter in an 18 cm heavy-based frying pan. Add a quarter of the potato to pan and cook for 6–7 minutes each side over low–medium heat until crisp and golden brown. Transfer latke to a baking tray and keep warm in oven. Add another tablespoon of clarified butter and cook another quarter of the potato. Repeat with remaining butter and potato to make 4 latkes.

For the apples, heat 1 tablespoon clarified butter in a frying pan, add apples and sauté over low–medium high heat until they are tender and caramelised.

Serve latkes with apples, coppa and a spoonful of crème fraîche or sour cream.

Braised zucchini, artichoke and borlotti beans with herbs

Serves 6

One of the most satisfying things about cooking from a garden is taking a vegetable that many would relegate to the compost pile or feed to the pigs, such as overgrown zucchini, and transforming it into a dish so sublime you actually leave a few to metamorphose on purpose. Large zucchini are only less pleasant to eat because they contain so much water, which dilutes their flavour. Here the liquid extracted from the zucchini during cooking is used to braise them with other vegetables and then reduced at the end, resulting in a rich flavourful sauce. Fresh borlotti beans are easy to grow and add a meatiness to the braise, but almost any vegetables can be added, so use whatever you have to hand.

125 ml (½ cup) olive oil
2 brown onions, thinly sliced
6 cloves garlic, thinly sliced
sea salt and freshly ground black pepper
2 kg (about 3 large) zucchini (courgettes), cut into 5 cm chunks
5 globe artichokes, prepared (see page 23)
140 g (1 cup) shelled fresh borlotti beans (from about 300 g borlotti beans in pods)
1 tablespoon chopped tarragon
1 tablespoon chopped savory or thyme

Heat olive oil in a large deep saucepan over medium heat. Add onion and garlic and sauté gently until onion is soft and translucent, about 8 minutes. Season with salt and add zucchini, then cover and simmer gently until zucchini is very tender, about 45 minutes.

Add artichokes and beans and continue cooking until they are tender and liquid is reduced by half, about 20 minutes. Add herbs and adjust seasoning with salt and pepper.

Serve in bowls with plenty of crusty bread to mop up the juices.

Pumpkin, potato and walnut gratin

Serves 6

There is a sense of occasion about a gratin, perhaps because the dish is often presented at the table to share. A gratin also offers a wonderful opportunity to meld flavours, in this case an autumn harvest of pumpkin, potatoes and walnuts. I find the best gratins contain plenty of butter, cheese or cream, which serves to lengthen the flavour. Cream often gets a bad reputation from being overused – think of those heavy, cloying pasta dishes. Here the cream is absorbed as the gratin cooks, so the finished dish isn't swimming in cream, but you can lighten it further by replacing a little of the cream with stock or water, if you like.

2 tablespoons olive oil, plus extra for drizzling
6 brown onions, thinly sliced
300 ml pouring cream
2 cinnamon sticks
2 bay leaves
12 sage leaves
1 tablespoon dijon mustard
butter, for greasing
1.2 kg potatoes, washed
1.5 kg pumpkin, peeled and seeds removed
sea salt and freshly ground black pepper
100 g crusty bread, crusts removed and coarsely chopped
100 g walnuts

Heat olive oil in a frying pan over low heat. Add onions and a pinch of salt and sauté gently, stirring occasionally, until onions are caramelised, about 10–12 minutes. Remove from heat and set aside.

In a small saucepan, combine cream, cinnamon sticks, bay leaves, sage leaves and mustard. Place over low heat and slowly bring to the boil, then remove from heat and set aside.

Preheat oven to 190°C and brush a 4-litre-capacity baking dish with butter. Using a mandoline, thinly slice potatoes and pumpkin. Beginning with potato, alternately layer potato and pumpkin slices into dish, seasoning each potato layer with salt and pepper. Halfway through, drizzle vegetables with half of the infused cream and scatter with the caramelised onions, then continue with the rest of the potato and pumpkin. Pour the other half of the cream over the gratin, then cover with foil and bake until vegetables are tender when pierced with a skewer, about 1 hour.

Meanwhile, pulse bread in a food processor until chopped, add walnuts and pulse until pieces of bread and walnuts are roughly the same size.

Remove gratin from oven and discard foil. Scatter breadcrumb and walnut mixture evenly over vegetables and drizzle with a little extra olive oil, then bake for another 15 minutes or until top is crisp and golden. Serve immediately.

Honey-poached apple and jam puddings with hop custard

Serves 10

The Derwent Valley was once well known for its hops, and the legacy of this past is the wild hop vines that make their way along the fences, up the electricity poles and through the willow trees that line the riverbanks. The parts used are the female flowers or cones, which do in fact look rather like soft pine cones and have an aroma reminiscent of passionfruit, citrus, stone fruit or flowers. If you don't happen to have a hop vine in your backyard, dried hops can be purchased from home-brewing stores or online.

180 g (½ cup) honey
4 apples, such as granny smith or golden delicious
160 g soft unsalted butter, plus extra for greasing moulds
120 g (¾ cup) icing sugar
225 g (1½ cups) plain flour
½ teaspoon baking powder
½ teaspoon fine sea salt
100 ml milk
caster sugar, for coating moulds
80 g (¼ cup) jam of your choosing, such as raspberry, strawberry or apricot

hop custard
375 ml (1½ cups) milk
450 ml pouring cream
5 fresh or dried hop cones
6 egg yolks
150 g caster sugar

In a large saucepan, combine honey and 500 ml (2 cups) water and bring to a simmer over medium heat. Peel and core apples, trim top and bottom and then cut into 3 cm slices crossways. Add apple slices to pan, reduce heat to low and gently poach apples until tender, about 20 minutes. Remove apple slices and set aside, then keep on simmering to reduce liquid until thick and syrupy.

For hop custard, place milk, cream and hops in a saucepan. Bring to the boil over low–medium heat and simmer gently for a minute. Whisk egg yolks and sugar together in a bowl until thick and pale, then gradually whisk in hot cream mixture. Return to same pan and stir over low heat until custard thickens enough to coat the back of a wooden spoon. Do not boil. Remove from heat and strain through a fine sieve, leave to cool slightly then refrigerate until chilled. (Makes about 1 litre.)

Using an electric mixer, cream butter and icing sugar until pale and fluffy. Sieve together flour, baking powder and salt. Add one-third of flour to creamed butter and sugar, followed by half the milk, and stir to combine. Repeat with remaining flour and milk.

Brush ten 150 ml-capacity ovenproof dariole moulds with soft butter, then coat with caster sugar. Place an apple slice in the base of each mould, trimming to fit if necessary, then pour over a tablespoon of the reduced poaching syrup. Spoon in a little batter, place a teaspoonful of jam in the middle then top with more batter, ensuring there is at least 1 cm of space left at top of mould.

Place a steamer filled with water over high heat. When steaming, add puddings and cook for 20–30 minutes or until mixture springs back when lightly pressed. Alternatively, the puddings can be cooked in a water bath in the oven: preheat oven to 180°C, place puddings in a deep baking dish and carefully pour hot water into dish until it reaches halfway up sides of puddings. Cover with foil and bake for 30 minutes or until mixture springs back when lightly pressed.

Serve puddings immediately with hop custard.

Buckwheat crêpes with apple and chestnuts

Serves 6 (makes 12 crêpes)

An extremely pretty plant to grow in a garden, buckwheat has heart-shaped leaves and dozens of tiny pink flowers. Because buckwheat is actually not a grain but a seed, related to rhubarb and sorrel, it contains no gluten. Ground into a flour (which can be purchased from wholefood stores), it adds a distinctive nutty flavour to these crêpes. Although chestnuts are much loved by Europeans and Americans, they are still gaining in popularity here. I won't lie, they do take a bit of work and can be fiddly to peel, but their sweet earthiness is beguiling – and they're crumbled for this dish, so there's no need to worry if they're not perfectly peeled. Even better, you can buy peeled and frozen or cryovac-ed Australian chestnuts from delicatessens or online.

500 g chestnuts
300 g apples (about 2 apples), such as granny smith or golden delicious
30 g unsalted butter
100 g caster sugar
500 g mascarpone
1 teaspoon vanilla paste
1 egg yolk

buckwheat crêpes
2 eggs
2 egg yolks
500 ml (2 cups) milk
75 g unsalted butter, melted, plus extra for cooking
250 g plain flour, sifted
50 g buckwheat flour, sifted
25 g caster sugar

Preheat oven to 190°C. Using a small sharp knife, score a cross through the skin of each chestnut and place on a baking tray. Roast for 40 minutes then, while chestnuts are still warm, carefully peel off and discard skin. Roughly crumble chestnuts. Turn oven down to 100°C.

For buckwheat crêpes, whisk together eggs and egg yolks in a bowl, then whisk in milk and butter. Whisk in flours and sugar, then set aside to rest for 15 minutes.

Peel apples and cut into 1 cm dice. Heat butter in a small frying pan over medium heat, add apple and half the sugar and cook until light caramel in colour, then add chestnut pieces and toss to combine. Set aside in the oven to keep warm.

Whisk together mascarpone, vanilla, egg yolk and remaining sugar, and refrigerate until required.

Heat a crêpe pan or 25 cm frying pan over medium–high heat and brush with a little melted butter. Ladle about 3 tablespoons crêpe batter into the pan, swirl to just coat the base, then cook until set, about 1–2 minutes. Using a spatula to help, carefully flip crêpe and cook for a further minute. Transfer to a warm plate and keep warm in oven. Repeat with remaining batter, brushing the pan with a little more butter before cooking each crêpe.

To serve, spoon some mascarpone mixture into the centre of each crêpe, top with apple and chestnuts, then fold over.

Stuffed apple dumplings

Serves 6

These little dumplings can be whipped up in a jiffy, then all you need are some woollen socks and an open fire and your night will be complete. They are self-saucing, but do need to be served with some cream or ice cream or custard, if you happen to have some lurking at the back of the fridge.

560 g (3¾ cups) plain flour
1½ teaspoons fine sea salt
¾ teaspoon baking powder
220 g cold lard, chopped
6 small apples, such as granny smith or golden delicious
75 g (⅓ cup) sugar
2 tablespoons brown sugar
2 teaspoons ground cinnamon
vanilla ice cream or double cream, to serve

In a large bowl, combine flour, salt and baking powder. Add lard and use your fingertips to rub in until mixture resembles coarse breadcrumbs. Add 125 ml (½ cup) ice-cold water and stir until dough just comes together, then knead until smooth. Wrap in plastic film and set aside at room temperature for about 30 minutes.

Preheat oven to 180°C. Peel and core apples. Divide pastry into six and roll each piece out on a lightly floured surface into a rough triangle shape about 5 mm thick. Place an apple in the centre of each triangle with its core cavity facing up. Combine sugars and cinnamon and divide mixture evenly between the apples, spooning it into the core cavities.

Enclose apples in pastry, pressing edges together to seal, then trim and discard excess. Place each apple in a pie tin and cook in oven for 1 hour or until apples are tender and pastry is golden.

Serve warm with ice cream or cream.

Pear and fig semolina tart

Serves 12

The origins of this tart date back to my days working for Sam Vico at Caffe Bassano, in Griffith. Being a talented pastry chef, Sam served this tart in the caffe (along with a plethora of other goodies from his pasticceria next door. The semolina makes a creamy, smooth filling without the richness of a crème pâtissière, but with a better texture than a baked custard. Sam's incarnation – the one that got me hooked – had pears, peaches and raspberries. The combination of pear and figs used here is perfect for autumn; feel free to dabble with different fruit at other times of year.

3 pears, peeled and cut into 2 cm chunks
50 g unsalted butter
270 g caster sugar
500 ml (2 cups) milk
100 ml pouring cream
80 g (½ cup) fine semolina
5 egg yolks
1 teaspoon vanilla paste
30 ml cointreau
5 figs, halved lengthways
icing sugar, for dusting

shortcrust pastry
500 g plain flour
310 g soft unsalted butter
1 egg
3 egg yolks
200 g icing sugar
pinch of salt
finely grated rind of 1 lemon

For shortcrust pastry, place flour in a large bowl and, using your fingertips, rub in butter until mixture resembles coarse breadcrumbs. Make a well in the centre and add egg, egg yolks, icing sugar, salt and lemon rind. Mix with a wooden spoon to form a soft dough. Wrap in plastic film and refrigerate for 1 hour.

Place pears, butter and 110 g (½ cup) caster sugar in a large saucepan and cook over medium heat for 10 minutes or until fruit is just tender. Strain through a colander, discard liquid and leave pears to cool.

Using your hands, press pastry into a lightly greased 20 cm springform tin, lining the base and sides to a thickness of about 8 mm. Trim excess pastry, then refrigerate for 30 minutes.

Preheat oven to 180°C. Pour milk and cream into a saucepan and bring to the boil. Scatter over remaining 150 g (⅔ cup) caster sugar and the semolina and whisk to combine, then stir over low heat for 10 minutes. Remove from heat and stir through egg yolks, vanilla and cointreau. Add pears to semolina custard, then pour into chilled tart shell and arrange fig halves on top, cut-side up.

Bake tart until custard is firmly set and golden, about 1 hour and 10 minutes. Cool on a wire rack before serving, dusted with icing sugar.

Apple and plum crumble

Serves 6

As a child, my all-time-favourite dessert was apple crumble, and it still holds a special place in my heart. This is the adult version, with plums and red wine – not only do these enhance the flavour, they also produce the most wonderful deep purple colour. For the crumble itself, I love the crunchiness of demerara sugar and the richness of walnuts. One last thing: don't skimp on the cream!

1 kg apples, such as granny smith or golden delicious
160 ml red wine
800 g blood plums, stones removed, coarsely chopped
75 g sugar
150 g plain flour
120 g cold unsalted butter, chopped
90 g demerara sugar
¼ teaspoon fine sea salt
50 g walnuts, finely chopped
thick cream, to serve

Peel and core apples, then cut into 2 cm chunks and combine in a saucepan with red wine, plums and sugar. Place over medium–high heat and bring to a simmer, then cook for 20 minutes or until apples are tender and sauce is reduced and slightly thickened. Spoon mixture into a large baking dish.

Preheat oven to 200°C. Using your fingertips, rub together flour, butter, demerara sugar, salt and walnuts. Scatter over fruit mixture in baking dish and bake for 20–30 minutes or until golden.

Serve the crumble warm, with plenty of thick cream.

Quince tarte tatin

Serves 4

Every Christmas and birthday my wife Séverine insists that I am hard to buy presents for, although she always manages to find something great. In reality, it needn't be complicated, for my face always lights up when someone brings me gifts of fruit, especially quinces. Living where we do, we are blessed to be surrounded by old country properties with quince trees on their land – remnants of orchards which, in a good year, bear fruit in abundance. Because quinces preserve extremely well, this is never a problem: we've done everything from candying them to making jellies and jams, even juicing them as an addition to cider. Sadly, many people think of quinces as difficult to prepare, but they are actually super-simple to cook, just needing sugar, water and time. As they do take so long to cook, it's worth making a double or triple batch and preserving the remainder in sterilised jars, then you could feasibly make this tart at any time of year. Poached quince also makes a wonderful addition to breakfast porridge (see page 248) or muesli and yoghurt. You can buy gorgeous copper tarte tatin pans, but I find you can't beat a good solid cast-iron frying pan.

440 g (2 cups) sugar
1 vanilla bean, halved lengthways
2 quinces (about 700 g in total)
½ quantity rough puff pastry (see page 164)
***or* 500 g readymade all-butter puff pastry**

Preheat oven to 150°C. Combine sugar, vanilla bean and 500 ml (2 cups) water in a heavy-based flameproof casserole and stir over low heat until sugar has dissolved. Peel quinces and quarter lengthways, then slip fruit and peelings into the sugar syrup. Cover and cook in oven for 3 hours or until quince is deep burgundy in colour. Remove and set aside to cool in the poaching liquid.

When quince has cooled, use a sharp knife to remove core from each quarter. Arrange quince quarters in the base of an 18 cm diameter heavy-based ovenproof dish or cast-iron frying pan about 5 cm deep. Drizzle with 2 tablespoons of the poaching liquid.

Increase oven temperature to 200°C. On a lightly floured work surface, roll out puff pastry until it is about 5 mm thick. Trim to fit dish or pan, then use a fork to prick pastry all over. Place pastry over quince and tuck in edges. Bake for 40–45 minutes or until pastry is a deep golden colour.

Meanwhile, strain quince poaching syrup into a saucepan and reduce over high heat to a thick syrup.

Carefully invert tart onto a serving plate, brush with syrup and serve.

Walnut and cardamom scrolls

Makes 12

When we moved to Tasmania, we rediscovered walnuts. Freshly cracked from their shells, they are an entirely different beast: creamy and sweet, with loads of nutty goodness. We buy them from a lady in New Norfolk who has a gigantic tree over her driveway. Each autumn, as the walnuts ripen, she moves her car to safety so it's not damaged by the falling nuts.

Walnuts will store in their shell for over a year, but once cracked they need to be consumed quickly or the oils will go rancid – and, unfortunately, that is the fate of most prepacked nuts. The best way to store shelled walnuts is to freeze them in small packs and use them straight from the freezer.

2 teaspoons dried yeast
375 ml warm milk, plus 2 tablespoons extra
975 g plain flour
2 teaspoons ground cardamom
220 g (1 cup) caster sugar
260 g unsalted butter, softened
1½ teaspoons ground cinnamon
150 g walnut halves, toasted and coarsely chopped
1 egg
icing sugar, for dusting

Combine yeast and warm milk in a small bowl, stirring until yeast has dissolved. In a large bowl, combine flour, cardamom, half the sugar and 160 g of the butter. Pour in yeast and milk mixture, stirring to combine, then knead until mixture forms a smooth dough. Place dough in a clean bowl, cover with plastic film and place in a warm spot until dough has doubled in size, about 1 hour.

Turn out dough onto a lightly floured work surface and cut in half. Working with one half at a time, roll out to a rectangle about 45 cm × 35 cm. Spread half the remaining butter over the dough and scatter with half the remaining sugar and half the cinnamon and walnuts. Starting at one of the long sides, roll up dough tightly to form a log. Repeat with remaining dough, butter, sugar, cinnamon and walnuts to form a second log.

Line 1 large or 2 smaller baking trays with baking paper. Using a sharp knife, make five diagonal cuts in each log, facing in opposite directions, so you end up with six roughly pyramid-shaped pieces of dough. Place pyramids, pointed-end up, on the baking tray and press down to slightly flatten. Cover trays loosely with clean tea towels and set aside in a warm place to rise for about 1 hour or until doubled in size.

Preheat oven to 180°C. Whisk together egg and extra milk and brush over scrolls. Bake until golden, about 25 minutes, then serve warm or at room temperature, dusted with icing sugar.

Note
If you get befuddled by the pyramids, simply cut the logs of dough into slices and bake. They'll taste just as good.

Damson gin

Makes about 1.5 litres

Scattered along the roadsides around Lachlan are spindly trees which, every autumn, produce dark purple fruit the size of a very large grape or small prune. On further investigation, I was told these were damson plums, escapees of the old orchards, where they would be grown at the ends of rows and used to top up preserves when needed. Given that damsons are extremely tart when eaten raw, they are only really coveted by the birds . . . and now me. For, with the addition of sugar, alchemy turns these astringent stonefruit into the best-tasting jams, jellies, cordials, sauces and ice creams. They also make an excellent infusion for gin, as does their close relative the sloe – a more common infusion that is available commercially.

1 kg damsons
400 g sugar
1.5 litres gin

Wash and dry damsons well and remove any leaf litter. Using a needle, prick each fruit several times and place in a clean 3-litre-capacity jar. Scatter over sugar and shake well, then pour over gin. Seal jar and store, shaking well occasionally, to help sugar to dissolve.

In 6 months, the damson gin will be ready for drinking and can be strained off into separate bottles for yourself or as a gift. The boozy fruit can also be reserved (keep it in the fridge once it's drained from the gin) and used in puddings or eaten as they are.

— chapter four —

winter

TRUFFLES . SLOW-COOKING . CIDER
BONFIRES . WOOD-FIRED BREAD

This need not be the season to shut up shop in the kitchen garden: the brassicas and root vegetables planted in summer will be ready for harvest in the cooler months. Winter is also a time for planning – new beds, new tree plantings – and for buying seeds in preparation for the next growth cycle of the garden in spring.

Wintry weather offers the perfect excuse to stay close to the oven and try your hand at bread-making, or to huddle around a bonfire and cook outdoors.

Chicken soup

Serves 6

Soup for the soul, this is a simple, straightforward soup designed to warm you to the bone on a cold winter's day. A whole chicken is used to make the broth and its shredded meat is returned to the soup, which is then lightly thickened to give it a velvety texture. This is a good basic soup to build upon, say if you want to add herbs or vegetables to change the flavours slightly; I find the perfect addition from the herb garden is lovage, if you have it.

2 tablespoons olive oil
1.8 kg chicken, jointed into about 10 pieces – ask your butcher to do this
3 brown onions, finely chopped
3 cloves garlic, thinly sliced
3 stalks celery, finely chopped
3 carrots, finely chopped
2 bay leaves
½ bunch thyme
sea salt and freshly ground black pepper
50 g unsalted butter
50 g (⅓ cup) plain flour

Heat olive oil in a large saucepan or stockpot over high heat. Add chicken pieces and cook, turning often, until skin is golden brown, then remove and drain on paper towel.

Turn heat down to low, add onion and garlic and cook, stirring occasionally, until onion is very soft and tender, about 10 minutes. Increase heat to medium, add celery and carrot and sauté until just beginning to soften, about 5 minutes.

Return chicken to pan, then add bay leaves and thyme, along with 3 litres water. Bring to a simmer and cook for 1½ hours or until meat is falling from the bones.

Using a slotted spoon, transfer chicken from soup to a tray or large plate. Remove and shred chicken meat, then return to soup. Discard bones. Season soup to taste with salt and pepper. In a small bowl, rub butter into flour using your fingertips, then add small pieces to the soup, whisking well until lightly thickened.

Ladle soup into bowls and serve.

Clam chowder

Serves 6

I fell in love with clam chowder on a trip to the USA, where they do a couple of versions: this one, with a milk base, is the New England style. With no stock-making, this is really easy, but the clams add an intense salty seafood flavour. Treat yourself to a good-quality smoked speck or bacon for this – it will make all the difference.

2 kg clams
40 g unsalted butter
1 × 100 g piece speck or bacon, cut into 1 cm strips
1 brown onion, finely chopped
1 stalk celery, finely chopped
2 tablespoons plain flour
1 litre warm milk
200 g desiree potato (about 1), peeled and cut into 1 cm dice
sea salt and freshly ground white pepper

Tip clams into a large bowl of salted water and leave to stand for 10 minutes, then drain and rinse. Place a large heavy-based saucepan over high heat, add clams and cover with a lid. Cook for 3 minutes or until clams have opened. Strain clam juices through a fine sieve and set aside. Reserve a handful of clams in their shells, then remove clam meat from remaining shells.

Melt butter in a large saucepan over medium heat, add speck or bacon and sauté for 5 minutes or until crisp, then remove with a slotted spoon and drain on paper towel. Reduce heat to low, add onion and celery to pan and sauté, stirring occasionally, for 8 minutes or until soft. Sprinkle in flour and cook, stirring constantly, for 4–5 minutes.

Add clam juices to pan and stir until smooth, then add milk a little at a time, stirring until smooth between each addition, until all milk is incorporated. Add potato and simmer for 8 minutes or until potato is soft, then stir in clam meat and remove from heat. Season to taste with salt and pepper.

Ladle chowder into small bowls and serve sprinkled with crisp speck or bacon and the reserved clams in their shells.

Lobster broth with truffles

Serves 8 as a starter

As you can probably guess from the ingredients list, this soup isn't something you might casually whip up on a Tuesday night for dinner. Save it for a special occasion with special people. This recipe wrings every drop of flavour from the lobster shell and uses the meat as highlights of texture and flavour throughout. The truffle blends harmoniously, and although it feels very more-ish while you're eating it, the small serving size is actually plenty, as the flavours are so intense.

1 × 650–800 g uncooked lobster
2 tablespoons olive oil
1 onion, thinly sliced
2 carrots, finely chopped
1 stalk celery, finely chopped
1 teaspoon fennel seeds
1 clove garlic, thinly sliced
2 tablespoons tomato paste (purée)
50 g unsalted butter
50 g plain flour
black truffle, to taste or budget

Place lobster in a plastic bag in the freezer for 1 hour, where it will 'go to sleep'.

Preheat oven to 220°C. Using a sharp knife, halve lobster lengthways. Remove lobster meat and refrigerate until required. Place lobster shells on a baking tray and roast until deep orange in colour, about 15–20 minutes.

Heat olive oil in a large saucepan, add onion, carrot, celery, fennel seeds and garlic and sauté over low heat for 10 minutes, then stir in tomato paste and sauté for a further 2–3 minutes. Add lobster shells and use a wooden spoon to coarsely crush them. Cover with 2.5 litres water. Bring to the boil over high heat, then reduce heat to low and simmer for 1½ hours.

Strain stock through a fine sieve and return to pan, then bring to a simmer. In a small bowl, rub butter into flour using your fingertips and add small pieces to the simmering stock, whisking well until lightly thickened. Remove from heat, then finely grate in black truffle and stir through.

To serve, thinly slice lobster meat and divide among bowls. Ladle over broth and serve immediately, scattered with extra shaved truffle.

Chicory and bacon on wet polenta with walnuts

Serves 4

Chicory is the cold-weather equivalent of lettuce – something crisp and refreshing to offset a meaty braise. The characteristic bitterness of chicory, which is muted by the winter chill, also serves a higher purpose, helping our bodies to digest the rich foods of winter. In this dish various chicory leaves are teamed with soft polenta. At The Agrarian Kitchen we are lucky to be able to grind our own polenta from home-grown corn, which sends the corn flavour off the scale. Unless you are really pushed for time, I recommend traditional polenta over the instant version, which is pre-cooked and tends to be blander in flavour with less texture. This dish makes a lovely starter or a side dish to go with a beautifully chargrilled medium-rare steak.

1 tablespoon olive oil
1 × 300 g piece smoked bacon, cut into 1 cm strips
100 g (1 cup) walnuts, coarsely chopped
2 tablespoons red wine vinegar
1 tablespoon brown sugar
400 g mixed chicory leaves, such as radicchio, witlof and endive
finely grated parmesan, to serve

wet polenta
300 ml milk
115 g polenta
60 g finely grated parmesan
sea salt and freshly ground black pepper

For wet polenta, combine milk and 300 ml water in a heavy-based saucepan and bring to a simmer over medium–high heat. Whisk in polenta, then reduce heat to low and stir using a wooden spoon until mixture is smooth and not gritty, about 1 hour. Stir in parmesan and season to taste with salt and pepper.

Heat olive oil in a frying pan, add bacon and walnuts and sauté over medium heat until bacon is browned and walnuts are toasted. Add vinegar and sugar and stir over heat to dissolve sugar.

To serve, spoon polenta onto plates, scatter with chicory leaves and spoon over bacon and walnut dressing. Serve immediately, with plenty of grated parmesan.

Fisherman's pie

Serves 6

It is dishes such as this that make me look forward to winter. It's easy to make, and can be cooked in individual dishes or as a large pie to share. Any seafood you like the look of at the fishmonger can be used, including salmon, squid, crab, clams or abalone – try to mix it up a little for a range of tastes and textures in the finished pie. I encourage you to make your own stock for the sauce: just ask your fishmonger for some bones, put them in a pot with celery, onion and bay leaves cover the lot with water and simmer gently for 30 minutes . . . simply strain and that's it!

1 kg black mussels, scrubbed and debearded
375 ml (1½ cups) fish stock
150 g unsalted butter
75 g (½ cup) plain flour
500 ml (2 cups) warm milk
10 g dried wakame seaweed
sea salt and freshly ground black pepper
220 g uncooked lobster tail meat or crabmeat
780 g white-fleshed fish, such as blue-eye trevalla or striped trumpeter

potato crust
1 kg medium-sized floury potatoes
fine sea salt
100 g unsalted butter, cut into small pieces
60 ml (¼ cup) pouring cream
150 ml milk

For potato crust, place unpeeled potatoes in a large saucepan, cover with cold water and add a pinch of salt. Bring to the boil, then reduce heat and simmer until potatoes are tender when pierced with a skewer, about 20 minutes. Drain potatoes and, when just cool enough to handle, peel and pass through a potato ricer or mash. Return potato to saucepan, add butter, cream and milk and stir over medium heat until smooth. Season to taste with salt and set aside.

Heat a large saucepan over high heat, add mussels and cover with a lid. Cook until mussels have opened, about 1–2 minutes. Strain mussel juices through a fine sieve and set aside. When cool enough to handle, remove mussels from shells and discard shells. Combine mussel juices and fish stock in a measuring jug, adding water if required to make 500 ml (2 cups) liquid.

For béchamel sauce, heat 90 g butter in a medium-sized saucepan over medium–high heat until butter is foaming. Add flour and stir until combined. Remove pan from heat, add a little warm milk and whisk to combine, then slowly add the rest of the milk and the fish stock mixture, whisking to ensure there are no lumps. Return to low–medium heat and bring to the boil, stirring constantly. Cook béchamel sauce for about 3–4 minutes to thicken, then stir through wakame and season to taste with salt and pepper. Leave to cool to room temperature.

Preheat oven to 180°C.

Using a sharp knife, cut lobster and fish into 2 cm pieces and combine with mussels. Add to cooled béchamel sauce and spoon into a 1.8-litre-capacity baking dish. Cover with spoonfuls of potato crust and dot with remaining butter.

Bake the pie until potato is golden, about 40 minutes, then serve immediately.

Fried tripe and chickpea salad

Serves 4

Tripe suffers from an image problem. Unfortunately, a whole generation has been scarred by being forced to eat tripe floating in a gluggy white sauce. The first time I ever ate tripe, it was cooked by Tetsuya Wakuda – I was working for him at the time – so unsurprisingly I was a convert from the start. The thing to remember when cooking tripe is that it has no real taste of its own, so you can bombard it with whatever flavours you like; it has a chewy texture, like calamari, so braise it until tender and it will suck up all those flavours. Then, for a textural treat, dust it in potato flour and fry it until crisp, as I've done here. Potato flour or starch is beautifully fine and silky – look for it in Asian stores.

200 g (1 cup) dried chickpeas, soaked overnight in cold water
400 g honeycomb tripe, cut into 1 cm strips
2 teaspoons fennel seeds
3 sprigs rosemary
6 juniper berries
2 bay leaves
2 carrots, peeled
1 celery heart
large handful flat-leaf parsley leaves
fennel fronds (optional)
vegetable oil, for deep-frying
150 g (1 cup) potato starch
sea salt

rosemary and garlic dressing
3 cloves garlic, peeled
1 sprig rosemary, leaves picked
sea salt
1 tablespoon seeded mustard
1 tablespoon white wine vinegar
60 ml (¼ cup) extra virgin olive oil
freshly ground black pepper

In a large saucepan, combine drained chickpeas, tripe, fennel seeds, rosemary, juniper and bay leaves. Cover with water and bring to the boil over high heat, reduce heat and simmer until chickpeas are tender, about 40 minutes. Drain and remove tripe pieces.

Using a mandoline or sharp knife, thinly slice carrots and celery heart lengthways. Place in a large bowl and add chickpeas, parsley leaves and fennel fronds, if using.

For rosemary and garlic dressing, place garlic cloves and rosemary leaves in a mortar with a pinch of sea salt and grind to a smooth paste with the pestle. Add mustard and vinegar and stir to combine, then whisk in olive oil and season to taste with salt and pepper.

Heat vegetable oil in a deep-fryer or large deep saucepan to 180°C. Pat tripe dry with paper towel and dust with potato starch, then deep-fry in batches for 4–5 minutes or until crisp. Season with sea salt.

Add tripe and dressing to bowl of vegetables and chickpeas and toss to combine, then serve immediately.

Bollito misto

Serves 10

Bollito misto is a grand affair, a winter ceremony to enjoy with a large group of friends. The name translates as 'mixed boiled', which in itself may not sound appealing, but the combination of different meats – usually beef, chicken, veal and cotechino sausage – is more than the sum of its parts. Available from Italian butchers and delis (or you might like to try making your own), cotechino is a heavily spiced, large pork sausage with a wonderful gelatinous texture from the pork skin in the filling.

1.8 kg beef brisket, rolled and tied
1 beef tongue (about 1.2 kg)
sea salt
1 teaspoon black peppercorns
1 cinnamon stick
2 bay leaves
12 small carrots, scrubbed
4 celery hearts, halved lengthways
2 brown onions, halved lengthways
1 cotechino sausage
1 × 1.6 kg organic chicken
freshly ground black pepper
mustard fruits, to serve

salsa verde
large handful flat-leaf parsley leaves
2 teaspoons rosemary leaves
3 anchovy fillets
2 garlic cloves
1 tablespoon small salted capers, rinsed
1 tablespoon red wine vinegar
60 ml (¼ cup) extra virgin olive oil

Place beef brisket and tongue in a large saucepan or stockpot. Cover with water and add a generous pinch of salt, the peppercorns, cinnamon stick, bay leaves, 2 carrots, 3 celery heart halves and 1 onion. Bring to the boil, then reduce to a gentle simmer and cook, skimming surface occasionally, until brisket and tongue are both tender, about 3 hours.

To cook cotechino, place sausage, still in its plastic wrapper, in a saucepan of cold water. Bring to the boil and simmer for about 1 hour or according to package directions.

Meanwhile, place chicken in a large saucepan and cover with cold water. Add a good pinch of salt, 2 carrots, ½ celery heart and the remaining onion. Bring to the boil, then reduce heat to a gentle simmer and cook for 40 minutes. Remove from heat and leave chicken to stand in broth for 20 minutes. Strain, reserving both chicken and broth.

Ladle a little of the chicken broth into a separate saucepan, season to taste with salt and pepper and bring to a simmer. Add remaining carrots and celery hearts and cook until tender, about 20 minutes.

Meanwhile, make salsa verde. Finely chop herbs, anchovies and garlic, then place in a bowl and stir through capers, vinegar and olive oil. Season to taste.

Serve meats on a large platter with vegetables and broth alongside, to be ladled over as desired. Carve meats at the table and serve accompaniments separately, including mustard fruits and salsa verde.

Sausage-stuffed beef brisket with horseradish cream

Brisket is a wonderful cut from the forequarter of beef that is greatly under-appreciated in this country. Perfect for slow-cooking, its wide, flat shape lends itself to stuffing. For this recipe the stuffing is quick and simple, yet packs a wonderful depth of flavour that permeates the meat. The sliced meat also makes a great sandwich the next day between two pieces of ciabatta.

1.2 kg beef brisket
sea salt and freshly ground black pepper
1 tablespoon olive oil

sausage stuffing
1 tablespoon olive oil
1 onion, finely chopped
3 cloves garlic, thinly sliced
1 carrot, finely diced
2 teaspoons fennel seeds
140 g (2 cups) fresh breadcrumbs
2 tablespoons finely chopped sage
500 g pork and fennel sausages
freshly ground black pepper

horseradish cream
250 ml (1 cup) sour cream or crème fraîche
2 tablespoons finely grated fresh horseradish or bottled horseradish
sea salt and freshly ground black pepper

For sausage stuffing, heat olive oil in a frying pan over low heat, add onion and garlic and sauté until beginning to caramelise, about 10 minutes. Add carrot and fennel seeds and cook, stirring occasionally, until carrot is tender. Stir through breadcrumbs and sage and set aside to cool. Remove sausage meat from skins and add to breadcrumb mixture, then season with pepper and combine everything well.

Preheat oven to 150°C. Place brisket on a chopping board and, using a long, sharp knife, cut a deep pocket in the longest side. Spoon in stuffing and, using kitchen string, truss brisket pocket closed. Season brisket with salt and pepper. Heat olive oil in a large frying pan over high heat, add brisket and sear each side until golden brown. Transfer to a roasting tin and roast for 2½–3 hours or until brisket is very tender.

Meanwhile, for horseradish cream, combine sour cream or crème fraîche and horseradish, then season to taste with salt and pepper.

Carve brisket into 1 cm slices and serve with horseradish cream.

Venison curry with flaky flatbread

Serves 6

This Indian-style curry is as straightforward as they get, with everything cooked together in one pot. The only exception is the shallots, which are fried and ground to a powder first – but if I'm in a big hurry I just grind up some of the packaged fried shallots you can get at Asian grocers.

9 cloves garlic, peeled
1.5 kg venison shoulder, cut into 3 cm pieces
1.1 kg (4 cups) plain yoghurt
1 tablespoon cardamom pods
1 tablespoon ground coriander
1 tablespoon black peppercorns
2 teaspoons cumin seeds
2 teaspoons chilli powder
1 teaspoon whole cloves
7 cm piece ginger, cut into fine strips
2 teaspoons sea salt
750 ml (3 cups) sunflower oil
6 golden shallots, thinly sliced
thick plain yoghurt and coriander sprigs, to serve

flaky flatbread
400 g plain flour, plus extra for dusting
100 g wholewheat flour
pinch of bicarbonate of soda
pinch of cream of tartar
1 teaspoon sugar
¾ teaspoon fine sea salt
60 ml (¼ cup) vegetable oil
1 egg
220 ml buttermilk
50 g unsalted butter, melted

Place garlic cloves in a blender, add 60 ml (¼ cup) water and blend until smooth. Pour garlic paste into a large heavy-based saucepan and add venison, yoghurt, spices, ginger, salt and 160 ml (⅔ cup) sunflower oil. Place over high heat and stir until mixture comes to the boil, then reduce to a simmer. Cook, stirring occasionally to scrape up browned bits from bottom of pan, until meat is tender, about 2 hours.

Heat remaining oil in a large saucepan or deep-fryer to 170°C. Add shallots and deep-fry until crisp and golden, about 2 minutes. Using a slotted spoon, remove shallots and drain on paper towel. When cool, place in a mortar and grind coarsely with the pestle. Add ground shallots and 500 ml (2 cups) water to venison and cook over medium heat until sauce is reduced and thickened, about 45 minutes.

For flaky flatbread, sift flours, bicarbonate of soda and cream of tartar into a large bowl. Stir in sugar and salt, then make a well in the centre. Add oil and egg and, using a fork, whisk to combine, then start to incorporate flour, gradually adding buttermilk and just enough water (about 1½ tablespoons) to make a soft dough. Knead dough until smooth, about 10 minutes, then cover with a clean tea towel and set aside for 10 minutes.

Divide dough into 12 and roll each piece into a ball. Dust lightly with flour and cover with the tea towel, then leave to rest for 30 minutes. Roll out each ball into a circle about 18 cm in diameter. Brush with melted butter, dust lightly with flour and fold in half, then brush with butter and dust with flour again and fold in half once more. Continue until all dough balls have been rolled and folded in this way, then roll out each one to about 3 mm thick. Heat a cast-iron or other heavy-based frying pan over medium heat and cook the flatbreads for 2–3 minutes each side, until puffed-up and speckled golden-brown.

To serve, spoon some venison curry into a flaky flatbread and top with a dollop of thick yoghurt and some coriander sprigs.

Pheasant braised in cider

Serves 6–8

I am lucky enough to have a wonderful source of pheasant throughout winter, and I have come to appreciate how special they really are. Your best bet is to order through a specialist game supplier in the major cities, or your butcher may be able to find them. They are leaner than chicken, but for this recipe chicken also works well.

2 × 1 kg pheasants, each cut into 6 pieces
180 ml (¾ cup) extra virgin olive oil
4 brown onions
2 tablespoons chopped thyme
4 bay leaves
4 cloves garlic, finely chopped
500 ml (2 cups) apple or pear cider
1 litre (4 cups) hot chicken stock
sea salt and freshly ground black pepper

garlic and parsley marinade
6 cloves garlic, peeled
3 handfuls flat-leaf parsley leaves
150 ml extra virgin olive oil

For garlic and parsley marinade, place garlic, parsley and olive oil in a small blender and process to a fine paste. Place pheasant pieces in a large bowl and season well with sea salt. Pour over garlic and parsley marinade and rub into pheasant. Cover and refrigerate for 2–3 hours.

In a large heavy-based frying pan, heat 125 ml (½ cup) olive oil over medium–high heat. Add pheasant and cook, turning occasionally, until golden brown on all sides. Transfer pheasant to a plate, then discard oil from pan and scrape clean. Add remaining olive oil to pan and gently sauté onion, thyme, bay leaves and garlic over low–medium heat for about 20 minutes until onion starts to brown.

Increase heat to high and return pheasant to pan. When pan is sizzling, add cider and scrape the bottom of the pan with a wooden spoon. Allow cider to bubble for 1 minute, then add stock and bring to the boil. Reduce heat to low, cover pan and simmer gently for 1 hour or until pheasant is very tender and almost falling from the bone.

If sauce has not reduced enough to coat the back of a spoon, remove pheasant and cook sauce over high heat to reduce further. Season to taste with salt and pepper and serve immediately.

The cider house rules

Not long after we moved to Lachlan I met the Nicholsons, who own a wonderful old property in the valley. Tony Nicholson is incredibly passionate about cider. During World War II, his cousin held a licence to brew cider locally, and further afield the craft has been practised across the valley for generations. Tony originally learnt the art of brewing wild-ferment cider from his father, and still brews small batches for home use.

It has become a yearly tradition for us to pick the apples together, before crushing and pressing them in Tony's old oasthouse. The resulting juice is allowed to settle before being decanted into wooden barrels where it ferments from the wild yeasts found on the apples and in the surrounding environment. Although wild yeasts can be unpredictable, they yield a far more interesting result. I find cultured cider yeasts are particularly harsh, often stripping out the flavour of the apples and producing a cider that lacks character.

The cider slowly bubbles away in the barrels until the brew finishes of its own accord – the timing will vary, depending on the weather. It is this wild fermentation that results in a cider that still tastes of apples with a wonderfully deep and earthy flavour; there may also be a slight hint of vanillin oak from the barrels, particularly if they happen to be new. The cider is bottled with a little sugar and corked or capped, before the final ingredient works its magic: time, in liberal doses.

The origins of cider are similar to beer. A working man's drink, it was often drunk in the fields. Since then, it has also become a wonderful ritual for the self-sufficient, a way to conserve excess apples that would otherwise rot – the trick is to make enough to last until the next year's brew is ready . . .

Cider apples have long been grown in the Derwent Valley.

The wooden crusher, made by Tony's father, breaks down the apples to a coarse pulp, which is then pressed in the old basket press.

Tony Nicholson's ancestors originally came from Herefordshire, so I suspect cider-making is in his blood.

Salt pork belly with sauerkraut

Serves 6

Salting pork in this way creates what is known as green bacon, which can be sliced and pan-fried with bacon-like results, sans the smokiness. It is a wonderful way to prolong the life of fresh pork, though you'll need to allow several days for the magic to happen. This recipe is a very simple way to enjoy this style of pork, traditionally served with sauerkraut and mustard. Add a glass of cider or ale and your winter wonderland is complete.

1.7 kg piece of pork belly
4 cloves
2 bay leaves
2 teaspoons black peppercorns
900 g sauerkraut
350 ml apple cider
dijon mustard, to serve

curing salt
500 g fine sea salt
100 g brown sugar
3 bay leaves
2 tablespoons coriander seeds
1 tablespoon black peppercorns
6 juniper berries
3 cloves

For curing salt, combine salt and sugar in a bowl. Place bay leaves, coriander seeds, peppercorns, juniper berries and cloves in a mortar and coarsely crush with the pestle. Add to salt and sugar and mix to combine. Curing salt can be stored in an airtight jar in the pantry for several months.

Pat pork belly dry with paper towel and place in a plastic container – pork may be cut to fit container, if necessary. Rub half the curing salt into pork belly, then cover and refrigerate overnight. Drain any liquid that has accumulated in the bottom of the container, rub pork belly with remaining curing salt and refrigerate for 2 days.

Remove pork from container and rinse off salt, then pat dry with paper towel. Place pork in a large saucepan, cover with water and add cloves, bay leaves and peppercorns. Bring to the boil over high heat, then reduce heat until water is just simmering and cook until pork is tender, about 2 hours.

Combine sauerkraut and cider in a saucepan and stir over medium heat until sauerkraut is warm and cider is reduced and syrupy, about 10 minutes.

Serve thick slices of pork belly on sauerkraut with mustard.

Pork and truffle sausage with truffled mash

Serves 6

A good sausage cannot be made and consumed on the same day, so allow yourself a couple of days. Each time the meat is worked it needs to be chilled again, to prevent the fat from warming and smearing through the meat; if this does happen, all the fat will run out of the sausages in the pan, resulting in a dry, mealy texture. Once the sausages are made, leave them to dry, uncovered and hanging in the fridge, for at least 3 hours but preferably overnight – this will prevent the skin from splitting during cooking.

1.6 kg pork shoulder meat, cut into 2 cm pieces
200 g pork back fat, cut into 2 cm pieces
40 g finely grated black truffle
30 g fine sea salt
freshly ground black pepper
1 hog casing, soaked overnight in cold water
olive oil, for frying

truffled potato mash

1 kg dutch cream potatoes
300 ml pouring cream
150 ml milk
finely grated black truffle, to taste or budget
80 g unsalted butter
sea salt and freshly ground black pepper

Mince pork meat and back fat through a coarse plate on a mincer, or ask your butcher to do this for you. Place in a bowl with black truffle and salt and use your hands to mix until well combined. To check the seasoning, cook a tablespoon of the mixture in a little oil in a frying pan and add more salt, if desired, and some pepper. Cover and chill mixture overnight.

Stuff meat into skins using a sausage stuffer or piping bag and twist into desired lengths. Refrigerate stuffed sausages for at least 3 hours – this dries out the skin slightly and prevents the sausage splitting when cooked. (The uncooked sausages will keep for up to a week in the fridge.)

For truffled potato mash, place potatoes in a large saucepan and cover with cold water. Add a pinch of salt and bring to the boil over high heat, then reduce heat and simmer until potatoes are tender when pierced with a skewer, about 20 minutes.

Meanwhile, cook the sausages. Heat a little olive oil in a large, heavy-based frying pan over low–medium heat, add sausages and cook gently, turning occasionally, for 15 minutes or until just cooked through.

When potatoes are cooked, drain through a colander and leave for 5 minutes to allow steam to escape. When just cool enough to handle, peel potatoes and pass through a potato ricer or mash. Heat cream, milk and truffle in a medium-sized saucepan until warm, then stir in potato. Add butter a little at a time, stirring well between each addition, then season to taste with salt and pepper.

Serve sausages on truffled potato mash, drizzled with pan juices – and with extra shavings of truffle, if desired.

Barbecue pork shoulder

Serves 8–10

Nothing is as good as a proper piece of barbecued pork, but this goes part-way towards trying to emulate those flavours without investing in a Texan smoker. The spice rub makes more than you need for this recipe, but it keeps for ages and is versatile enough to use with any meat. The sauce is also superb on many things, and you'll soon find yourself slathering it over everything that comes across your plate.

3 kg pork shoulder on the bone
2 teaspoons olive oil
coleslaw (see page 229), to serve

barbecue spice rub
165 g (¾ cup) fine sea salt
220 g (1 cup) brown sugar
2 teaspoons ground fennel
3 teaspoons cumin seeds
40 g (⅓ cup) sweet smoked paprika
1 tablespoon dried oregano
1 tablespoon chilli flakes
2 teaspoons mustard powder
1 teaspoon celery seeds
1 tablespoon ground allspice
2 teaspoons ground ginger
2 tablespoons fried shallots, ground
2 teaspoons freshly ground black pepper

barbecue sauce
250 ml (1 cup) tomato ketchup
125 ml (½ cup) blackstrap molasses
60 ml (¼ cup) apple cider vinegar
1 teaspoon tabasco sauce
¼ teaspoon ground allspice
¼ teaspoon ground cinnamon
¼ teaspoon ground mace
¼ teaspoon ground black pepper
½ teaspoon chilli flakes
½ teaspoon sweet smoked paprika

For barbecue sauce, combine all ingredients in a saucepan and stir constantly over medium heat until sauce comes to a simmer. Cook for 5 minutes, then set aside to cool.

For barbecue spice rub, combine all ingredients in a bowl and mix well. Spoon mixture into an airtight container and store in a cool place until required.

Preheat oven to 130°C. Score the pork skin at 1 cm intervals with a sharp kitchen knife or stanley knife. Place pork in a roasting tin and evenly coat with most of the spice rub, pushing it well into the scorelines. Cook in oven for about 5 hours or until meat is very tender and pulls easily away from the bone.

To serve, coarsely shred the pork and serve with barbecue sauce, coleslaw and remaining spice rub on the side.

Note
Any leftover barbecue sauce can be bottled and kept in the fridge for several months.

Coleslaw

Serves 8

I grew up with coleslaw quite unlike the recipe below. My experience was shaved cabbage and carrots – yep, that's the same – but there the similarity ends, for the Australian version would be swimming in sickly sweet mayonnaise. The traditional American version, designed to cut through the rich smokiness of barbecued meats, is made with a vinegar-based dressing and the cabbage is first salted to draw out moisture, allowing it to suck up the dressing. Make this salad a regular part of your winter table.

900 g white cabbage
2 turnips, cut into fine julienne strips
1 carrot, cut into fine julienne strips
sea salt
60 ml (¼ cup) double cream
60 ml (¼ cup) sour cream
4 spring onions, thinly sliced
freshly ground black pepper

dressing
125 ml (½ cup) apple cider vinegar
110 g (½ cup) caster sugar
½ teaspoon sea salt
1 tablespoon dijon mustard
60 ml (¼ cup) peanut oil

Using a mandoline, finely shred cabbage. Place in a bowl and add turnip, carrot and 2 tablespoons sea salt. Leave to stand at room temperature for at least 30 minutes or until wilted, then use your hands to squeeze out any excess liquid.

For dressing, combine vinegar, sugar and salt in a non-reactive saucepan. Bring to the boil over medium heat, then reduce heat and simmer, stirring occasionally, for 3 minutes. Remove from heat, then whisk in mustard and oil.

Pour warm dressing over vegetables and stir well to combine. Leave to cool, then stir through creams and spring onion. Season to taste with salt and pepper, then refrigerate until required. If possible, leave coleslaw in fridge overnight before serving, to allow the vegetables to absorb the flavour of the dressing.

Baked beans

Serves 6

Proper baked beans seem to be popping up on cafe menus everywhere. They are simple to prepare as long as you remember to soak the beans overnight and, once you've made a large pot, they can be refrigerated and reheated when required. They are wonderful with a poached or fried egg on top. They have become a staple part of our 'Whole Hog' class, served as breakfast on the second day. We utilise the pork bones, roasting them first and then cooking them with the beans, so they give up those last morsels of sweet meat nestled close to the bone.

2 tablespoons olive oil
1 onion, thinly sliced
3 cloves garlic, thinly sliced
2 × 400 g cans chopped tomatoes
400 g (2 cups) dried haricot or other white beans, soaked overnight in cold water
75 g (⅓ cup) brown sugar
2 tablespoons apple cider vinegar
1 tablespoon dijon mustard
2 tablespoons hot smoked paprika
1 teaspoon chilli flakes
1 teaspoon ground cloves
1 teaspoon ground fennel
1 teaspoon ground cinnamon
2 tablespoons blackstrap molasses
1 kg bacon bones *or* 1 smoked pork hock
sea salt and freshly ground black pepper
toast, to serve

Preheat oven to 160°C.

Heat olive oil in a large flameproof casserole over medium heat. Add onion and garlic and cook, stirring continuously, for 8 minutes or until soft, then add all remaining ingredients except salt and pepper and toast.

Pour in 1.5 litres water and bring to the boil, then cover and cook in oven for 4–5 hours or until beans are tender, stirring occasionally and adding more water as required.

Remove bacon bones or pork hock and shred meat from bones, then return meat to beans and discard bones.

Season beans to taste with salt and pepper, then gently reheat and serve with toast.

A winter bonfire

It is a primal instinct to cook with fire, though it is primarily a winter pursuit, when it serves the dual purpose of cooking and providing warmth. The open flame can be as simple as a fire in a grate indoors or a backyard barbecue, or as grand as a bonfire gathering with friends, where whole joints are roasted and gently simmering braises are nestled in the coals.

The smouldering embers of a bonfire slow-cook root vegetables to perfection.

Spiced cider

Serves 6

When staring into the flames of a bonfire it is crucial that you have a cup of warm liquid to sip. This spiced cider fits the bill. It is simple to throw together, though you may like to add or take away spices to your own taste – for instance, I was given a cardamom plant, which I carefully nurtured, and I discovered that a few choice leaves added to the pot only served to enhance the brew.

7 cm piece ginger, finely sliced
1 sprig thyme
300 ml apple juice
3 tablespoons brown sugar
2 cinnamon sticks
2 strips lemon rind
1 litre dry cider
100 ml brandy, or to taste

Place all ingredients in a large saucepan and stir over low–medium heat until very hot, but without letting it boil.

Ladle out spiced cider as required.

Fire-roasted onions with grilled leeks and soft eggs

Serves 6

I have developed a fondness for alliums (members of the onion family) which, when it comes to starring roles, are often overlooked in favour of the sexier vegetables. What most don't appreciate is the complexity that can be coaxed from them when their natural plant sugars are slowly caramelised. Fire-roasting is the perfect way of achieving this, as the smokiness is a great foil for the sweetness.

1.5 kg small onions or golden shallots
1 kg baby leeks
2 tablespoons olive oil
sea salt
6 chicken or duck eggs

cider sauce
200 ml cider vinegar
80 g unsalted butter
55 g (¼ cup) caster sugar
2 tablespoons chopped marjoram
sea salt and freshly ground black pepper

Place a grillplate over a well-developed fire with lots of hot embers. Using long-handled tongs, nestle the onions into the embers, then shovel over some more embers, ensuring onions are covered. When onions are tender, about 30–40 minutes, carefully remove and, when cool enough to handle, peel them.

Meanwhile, brush leeks with olive oil and season with sea salt. Place on grill and cook, turning often, until leeks are tender, about 10–15 minutes.

Bring a saucepan of water to the boil, add eggs and cook for 4 minutes. Remove from heat and plunge eggs into cold water, then peel.

For cider sauce, combine cider vinegar, butter and sugar in a small non-reactive saucepan. Place over the fire and stir until butter has melted and sugar has dissolved. Stir through marjoram, then season to taste with salt and pepper.

To serve, place onions on plates with leeks and soft-boiled eggs, then drizzle with cider sauce.

Buried root vegetable salad

Serves 10–12

This is probably the easiest recipe in the book . . . provided you take building and maintaining a fire out of the equation. The vegetables are basically cooked in the earth, which is wonderfully appropriate, since that is where they grow. The cooking time will depend on the coals, but it is better to start sooner than later – once they're ready, the vegetables can easily be left buried to stay warm. As they'll come out of the ground covered in dirt and ash, they do need to be peeled, but the skins should slip off easily. If you cook them in the oven, you can of course leave the skins on.

3.5 kg root vegetables, such as carrots, beetroot, salsify, jerusalem artichokes and turnips
sea salt and freshly ground black pepper

garlic mayonnaise
6 cloves garlic, peeled
sea salt
2 egg yolks
1 tablespoon dijon mustard
375 ml (1½ cups) extra virgin olive oil

Dig a hole near the edge of the fire or in the ashes at the edge of the fireplace. Shovel in a layer of hot coals then top with the unpeeled vegetables in a single layer. Carefully shovel in another layer of hot coals, then cover with a layer of ash or soil. Leave to cook for 1–2 hours, checking occasionally, until vegetables are tender. Remove vegetables and peel.

For garlic mayonnaise, place garlic in a mortar with a pinch of sea salt and crush to a fine paste with the pestle. Transfer garlic paste to a bowl and whisk in egg yolks and mustard. Slowly add olive oil in a thin steady stream, whisking constantly, until mayonnaise is thick and emsulsified, adding a little warm water if it becomes too thick. Season to taste with salt.

Season vegetables with salt and pepper and serve with garlic mayonnaise.

Spit-roast saddle of lamb with anchovies, rosemary and fennel

Serves 12

Roasting a whole lamb, while impressive, also poses problems – the main one being that the different parts require different cooking times. One way to overcome this is to just use the saddle, basically the mid-section of the lamb without the legs or shoulders. This will still yield enough meat to feed a small army and, most importantly, it will all be evenly cooked. The cooking time on a spit will vary widely, depending on its distance from the heat and how windy the conditions are. Of course the lamb can also be cooked in an oven, though it will probably need to be halved to fit.

1 deboned lamb saddle (about 5 kg)
3 tablespoons fennel seeds
2 bulbs garlic, cloves separated and peeled
finely grated rind of 3 lemons
15 anchovy fillets
small handful rosemary leaves
2 tablespoons sea salt flakes

Place lamb skin-side down on a clean work surface. Put fennel seeds into a mortar and coarsely crush with the pestle, then add remaining ingredients and pound to a rough paste. Smear paste over lamb, the roll up and secure with kitchen twine.

Thread spit pole through middle of the lamb, place over hot coals and set spit turning. The cooking time will depend on many factors, however cooking over coals should be done slowly: a best-case scenario would be 3–4 hours. A constant supply of hot coals from a separate fire will be a big help in maintaining a constant heat. The best way to check when the lamb is ready is using a meat thermometer – the internal temperature needs to reach 60°C for medium-rare, 65°C for medium.

Carefully remove lamb from spit. Cover loosely with foil and allow to rest for 20 minutes, then slice and serve.

Quince syrup dumplings

Serves 8

Apart from apple crumble, my other favourite childhood dessert would have to be golden syrup dumplings. This version poaches the dumplings in the quince-cooking syrup, which imparts an amazing flavour and a brilliant ruby-red colour. If you have access to a feijoa tree, its fruit is sublime poached together with the quince – and, serendipitously, both ripen at the same time. Feijoa is a member of the guava family and is also known as pineapple guava; its almost-tropical flavour is highly valued in our temperate climate.

1.32 kg (6 cups) sugar
2 vanilla beans, split lengthways
6 quinces, peeled and quartered
12 feijoas, peeled and halved lengthways (optional)
thick cream, to serve

dumplings
300 g (2 cups) self-raising flour
120 g cold unsalted butter, cubed
2 eggs
80 ml (⅓ cup) milk

In a large cast-iron or other heavy-based pan, combine sugar with 2 litres water. Add vanilla beans and stir over medium heat until sugar has dissolved, then add quince and cover. Place pan in the ashes at the edge of the fire and shovel embers around it. Ensure syrup is just below simmering point, then cook for 2 hours. Add feijoa, if using, and continue to cook until fruit is tender.

For dumplings, sift flour into a bowl. Using your fingertips, rub butter into flour until mixture resembles fine breadcrumbs. Beat eggs with milk and pour into flour mixture. Mix to form a dough, then shape into small balls.

Carefully slip dough balls into hot syrup, then cover pan and cook until dumplings are cooked through, about 20 minutes. When they are ready, they will have swelled to double their original size.

Serve dumplings with the fruit, some syrup and a good dollop of thick cream.

Marshmallows

Makes about 30

Marshmallow is essentially meringue set with gelatine – the version below is plain vanilla, but the flavours can be as wild and vivid as your imagination allows. Marshmallows are non-negotiable at a bonfire, for toasting and for making s'mores by smooshing the toasted marshmallows with a piece of chocolate between sweet plain biscuits.

500 g white sugar
1 tablespoon liquid glucose
2 tablespoons powdered gelatine
2 egg whites
1 tablespoon vanilla paste
80 g icing sugar
70 g cornflour

Place sugar, glucose and 200 ml water in a small saucepan and stir over low heat until sugar has dissolved. Increase heat to high and simmer, without stirring, until syrup reaches 121°C on a sugar thermometer ('hard ball' stage).

Meanwhile, sprinkle gelatine over 200 ml water in a small heatproof bowl and leave to stand for 10 minutes, then place over a saucepan of simmering water and stir until gelatine has dissolved. Carefully add gelatine to hot sugar syrup.

Using an electric mixer, whisk egg whites until stiff peaks form, then, with motor running, slowly pour in syrup. Add vanilla paste and whisk until well combined.

Combine icing sugar and cornflour in a small bowl. Line a 30 cm × 20 cm tin with baking paper and dust the base with half the icing sugar and cornflour. Pour in the marshmallow mixture, smooth the top with a spatula and allow to cool completely.

Using a knife dipped in hot water, cut marshmallow into 3 cm squares and dust with remaining icing sugar and cornflour.

Place a marshmallow on the end of a long stick and toast over fire until golden brown and gooey. Consume immediately.

Mixed-grain porridge with poached quince

Serves 4

There is no breakfast quite as satisfying in winter as porridge. This mixed-grain version came about as we were experimenting with our newly acquired grain-mill, but the rolled grains can all be purchased from wholefood stores or you can just use oats. For the creamiest porridge, soak the grains in water overnight and then cook them in full-cream milk. The acidity of cooked fruit is excellent with porridge – if not quinces, try bottled apricots, plums or peaches from the preserving shelf, or even good old stewed apple.

60 g flaked rye grains
150 g rolled oats
100 g rolled wheat
750 ml (3 cups) milk
sea salt
100 g walnuts, coarsely chopped
brown sugar and pouring cream, to serve

poached quince
2 quinces
220 g (1 cup) sugar
3 star anise

For poached quince, peel and quarter quinces. Remove cores and reserve. Combine sugar, star anise and 250 ml (1 cup) water in a saucepan and bring to a simmer to dissolve sugar. Add quinces and cores, cover and poach for 3 hours or until fruit is tender and deep-red in colour. Remove quince pieces, reserving quarters and discarding cores. Return syrup to heat and reduce over high heat until slightly thickened. Return quince to syrup and refrigerate until required.

Combine grains in a bowl, cover with water and set aside to soak overnight. The next morning, drain the soaked grains and transfer to a saucepan. Add milk and a pinch of salt, then stir over medium heat until porridge grains are tender, about 5–10 minutes.

Meanwhile, preheat oven to 180°C. Spread walnuts over a small tray and roast until golden, about 7 minutes.

Serve porridge in bowls, topped with quince. Scatter over the walnuts and brown sugar and drizzle with cream.

Baked egg custard with honey pears

Serves 6–8

Baked custard is comfort food. Sure, it can be cooked in individual dishes for an air of sophistication, but I think it is best shared from one large dish. Poached in honey syrup until tender, pears are an elegant fruit for winter desserts; the syrup takes on the pear flavour, which is concentrated further by reducing the syrup before serving.

750 ml (3 cups) milk
1 vanilla bean, split lengthways
3 duck eggs *or* 4 chicken eggs
6 duck egg yolks *or* 8 chicken egg yolks
250 g caster sugar
freshly grated nutmeg

honey pears
120 g (⅓ cup) honey
4 small pears (about 150 g each), peeled and halved lengthways
5 bay leaves

For honey pears, combine honey and 200 ml water in a medium-sized saucepan and bring to the boil. Add pears and bay leaves and reduce heat until barely simmering. Poach until pears are tender, about 1 hour. Using a slotted spoon, remove pears and set aside. Increase heat and simmer until poaching liquid has reduced to a syrup, then return pears to pan and turn to coat in syrup.

Preheat oven to 150°C. Combine milk and vanilla in a heavy-based saucepan over medium heat and bring to just below simmering point. Meanwhile, whisk together eggs, egg yolks and sugar in a large bowl, then pour over warm milk and stir to combine. Remove vanilla bean and scrape seeds into custard. Pour custard into a 1-litre-capacity ovenproof dish and scatter with nutmeg.

Cover dish with foil, stretching it taut, then carefully prick foil with a fork. Place dish in a roasting tin and fill tin with enough hot water to come halfway up the sides of the dish. Bake until custard is set but still wobbles in the centre, about 50 minutes.

Serve custard warm or cold with honey pears and syrup.

Truffle trifle

Serves 6

It might have been the way 'truffle trifle' rolls off the tongue that I loved initially – but, regardless, this sophisticated dish stands on its own merits. It was originally served at a special truffle lunch held at The Agrarian Kitchen, and was a real winner. As black truffles require fat to carry their flavour, they work brilliantly in dairy-rich desserts, manifesting as an earthy, cocoa-like flavour.

100 ml pedro ximenez sherry
320 g (1 cup) good-quality berry jam
500 ml (2 cups) pouring cream, whipped to soft peaks

milk granita
1 litre milk
110 g (½ cup) caster sugar
15 g finely grated black truffle

pastry cream
600 ml milk
1 vanilla bean, split lengthways
140 g caster sugar
15 g finely grated black truffle
120 g plain flour
60 g cold unsalted butter, chopped
90 g egg yolk (from about 5 eggs)

sponge cake
3 eggs
80 g caster sugar
1 teaspoon vanilla extract
75 g plain flour, plus extra for dusting
¼ teaspoon finely grated lemon rind
2 teaspoons melted butter

For milk granita, combine all ingredients in a small saucepan and stir over low–medium heat until sugar has dissolved. Pour mixture into a freezer-proof container and freeze until frozen solid, about 6 hours or overnight. Using a fork, scrape mixture into small ice crystals.

For pastry cream, place milk, vanilla bean and 40 g sugar in a small saucepan and bring to the boil. Place remaining sugar in a bowl with flour, then rub in butter with your fingertips to make a crumble. Add crumble to boiling milk and cook, stirring constantly, for 6 minutes, to cook the flour. Add egg yolk and truffle and cool by whisking at low speed in an electric mixer fitted with a paddle attachment.

For sponge cake, preheat oven to 180°C and lightly grease and flour a 20 cm round cake tin. Using an electric mixer, whisk eggs and sugar until thick and pale and doubled in volume. Add vanilla extract and whisk until just combined. Sift in one-third of flour and fold gently to combine. Sift in remaining flour, add lemon rind and melted butter and fold gently to combine. Pour mixture into prepared tin and bake for 40 minutes or until golden and centre springs back when lightly pressed. Leave to cool in tin for 20 minutes, then carefully remove tin and place cake on a wire rack to cool completely.

Cut sponge into 1 cm thick slices, place in the base of six serving bowls or glasses and drizzle with pedro ximenez sherry. Fold together pastry cream and whipped cream and spoon over sponge, then top with a spoonful of berry jam and some truffle milk granita. Finish with extra truffle shavings.

Note
This recipe makes more sponge cake than you need, but the remaining cake freezes well and can be used for future trifles.

Apple and rhubarb strudel with cardamom custard

Serves 6

Rhubarb tends to be our go-to fruit here. While the peak of ripeness for true fruits is often fleeting, rhubarb, unfazed by the changing seasons, stays stoically in the ground until harvested. Its flavour is transformed by sugar and it blends seamlessly with everything from stonefruit to apples and pears, berries to citrus. The trick to strudel pastry is to ever-so-gently stretch the pastry as thinly as possible – it may help to have two pairs of hands.

50 g unsalted butter, plus 75 g extra, melted, for brushing
100 g fresh breadcrumbs
800 g apples (such as gala, pink lady or granny smith), peeled, cored and thinly sliced
350 g rhubarb, trimmed and thinly sliced
125 g caster sugar
½ teaspoon ground cinnamon
icing sugar, for dusting

pastry
260 g (1¾ cups) white bread flour, plus extra for dusting
1 egg
55 ml vegetable oil
pinch of salt

cardamom custard
300 ml pouring cream
200 ml milk
4 cardamom pods, lightly cracked with the side of a knife
6 egg yolks
55 g (¼ cup) caster sugar
2 teaspoons cornflour

For pastry, combine flour, egg and oil with 60 ml (¼ cup) lukewarm water and a pinch of salt in the bowl of an electric mixer fitted with a dough hook. Knead on low speed until dough comes together, then transfer to a clean bowl, cover and leave to rest for 1–2 hours in a warm spot.

Heat butter in a large frying pan over medium heat until foaming, then add breadcrumbs and stir until golden. Tip toasted breadcrumbs into a large bowl and add apples, rhubarb, caster sugar and cinnamon and mix well.

Preheat oven to 190°C and line a large baking tray with baking paper. Lightly dust bench with flour and roll out dough until it is as thin as possible and measures approximately 60 cm × 40 cm. Gently slide pastry onto a clean, lightly floured tea towel. Spoon apple and rhubarb filling in a strip along the centre of the pastry, leaving about 10 cm space at each end. Fold ends over and then, using the tea towel to help, roll pastry tightly to enclose filling. Place strudel on prepared baking tray, brush with melted butter and bake for 35–40 minutes or until golden brown.

Meanwhile, for cardamom custard, place cream, milk and cardamom pods in a saucepan and bring to the boil. Whisk together egg yolks, sugar and cornflour in a bowl, then gently pour in warm milk mixture and whisk to combine. Return custard to saucepan and stir over low heat until mixture thickens, about 3–4 minutes. Strain to remove cardamom pods.

Dust strudel with icing sugar and serve slices with cardamom custard.

Bread-making

◇◇

Part art and part science, making your own bread is immensely satisfying. Nothing beats learning alongside a master bread-maker, but the following guidelines will help you to get started.

Good bread depends on good flour. If you're really keen, a grain mill is a worthwhile investment. Otherwise, for the freshest flour, seek out a supplier of flour milled from biodynamic or organic grains that has a high turnover. Bread flour (sometimes called strong flour) has a higher protein/gluten content, enabling it to develop a stronger structure and hold the gases given off by the yeasts as they ferment to give a nice light bread.

Some of the bread recipes we use at The Agrarian Kitchen include a pre-ferment stage, where a portion of the yeast and flour is mixed together to make a dough and then left to ferment overnight before being added to the final dough. This results in bread with better flavour, due to the long, slow rise of the pre-ferment.

Kneading the dough is what causes the gluten to develop and become stretchy; 'knocking back', a quick knead to deflate the dough once it has risen, also aids in this process. For the best results, knead your bread dough well and when knocking it back, follow the recipe instructions carefully.

Professional bread-makers tend to give the quantities of all ingredients in their recipes, including liquids, in grams. This not only makes for more accurate measurement, but also makes it easier to scale the recipe up or down.

The breads we make at The Agrarian Kitchen include what we call everyday bread, an airy ciabatta, a traditional German rye and a classic white loaf.

Everyday bread

Makes 2 loaves

All through winter we make this bread in our 'Agrarian Experience' classes and bake it in our wood-fired oven. A small amount of wholegrain wheat flour and rye flour gives the bread a nutty flavour. Bannetons, used for the bread's final rise, are cane baskets designed to allow loaves to keep their shape while they rise; they are available at good kitchenware stores or online. However, this bread can also be shaped and baked in loaf tins.

<u>**pre-ferment**</u>
⅛ teaspoon dried yeast
450 g bread flour
1½ teaspoons fine sea salt

270 g white bread flour, plus extra for dusting
90 g whole rye flour
90 g whole wheat flour
1 teaspoon fine sea salt
½ teaspoon dried yeast

For pre-ferment, stir yeast into 270 ml water in a large bowl, then add flour and salt and mix well. Cover and let stand for 12–16 hours. When it is ready, the pre-ferment will be domed and just beginning to recede in the centre.

In a large bowl or an electric mixer fitted with a dough hook, combine all remaining ingredients with 355 ml water and mix until dough just comes together. Add pre-ferment in chunks and knead until incorporated. The dough should be supple and loose. Cover dough with plastic film or a clean tea towel and set aside for 2–3 hours or until doubled in size, knocking it back once after 50 minutes, then again 50 minutes later.

Divide dough in half and shape into round or oval loaves. Place in floured bannetons or loaf tins, cover with a clean tea towel and leave to rise for about 1½ hours.

Preheat oven to 230°C and place a baking sheet in to heat. Invert loaves onto hot baking sheet (or, if using tins, simply slide them into the oven) and bake for about 30–40 minutes or until golden brown and hollow-sounding when tapped on base.

Ciabatta

Makes 2 loaves

Ciabatta dough is wet, very wet! It is the moisture and the fact that the air is not knocked out of the developing dough that give ciabatta its characteristic large holes. It is also imperative that the oven is super-hot. A baking or pizza stone (see page 148) will give the best results, as the dough starts cooking immediately on contact.

1½ teaspoons dried yeast
900 g white bread flour, plus extra for dusting
3 teaspoons sea salt
olive oil, for greasing
coarse semolina, for dusting

For pre-ferment, combine a scant ¼ teaspoon yeast and 250 ml (1 cup) water in a bowl and stir until yeast has dissolved, then add 200 g flour and stir until smooth. Cover bowl with plastic film and set aside for 12–16 hours or until foamy and doubled in size.

Place remaining flour and yeast, salt and 600 ml (2½ cups) water in an electric mixer fitted with a dough hook and mix on the lowest speed for 3 minutes or until dough comes together. With motor running, add pre-ferment in chunks and mix until well combined, then increase speed and mix for another 3 minutes, or until dough is smooth.

Place dough in an oiled bowl and turn to coat in oil. Cover bowl with plastic film and leave dough in a draught-free place for 1 hour or until doubled in size. Turn out dough onto a heavily floured work surface and, using floured hands, fold dough in half twice. Return dough to bowl, cover again and leave for 2 hours, then repeat folding.

Divide dough in half, then place on semolina-dusted baking trays and gently shape into loaves by tucking under the sides. Cover with a clean tea towel and leave to rise for 1½ hours or until doubled in size.

Preheat oven to 230°C. Bake ciabatta for 30–35 minutes or until golden and hollow-sounding when tapped on base.

German rye bread

Makes 1 loaf

The complex flavours of a wonderful, sour rye bread go perfectly with slices of smoked salmon or cured meats in general. These flavours are achieved by creating a starter. As rye doesn't have the same gluten content as wheat it doesn't create as light a loaf; a small amount of wheat flour is added here, to give the loaf some structure, but more can be added if you like your rye less dense – just reduce the amount of rye flour proportionately.

1½ teaspoons dried yeast
350 g rye flour
100 g white bread flour, plus extra for dusting
2 teaspoons fine sea salt

starter
½ teaspoon dried yeast
50 g white bread flour
1 tablespoon milk

For starter, combine yeast and 60 ml (¼ cup) water in a small bowl and stir until yeast has dissolved, then add flour and milk and stir until well combined. Cover with plastic film and leave to ferment for 12–18 hours or until bubbly and sour-smelling.

Place 250 ml (1 cup) water in a small bowl, sprinkle over yeast and leave for 5 minutes, then stir to dissolve. Combine flours in a large bowl and make a well in centre. Add dissolved yeast and fermented starter to well and stir in just enough flour to form a thick batter, leaving the rest of the flour piled against the sides of the bowl. Cover bowl with a clean tea towel and leave in a draught-free place for 12 hours, or until frothy.

Add salt and 100 ml water and stir in all the remaining flour from the sides of bowl to form a stiff dough. Turn out dough onto a lightly floured work surface and knead until smooth and elastic. Shape into a round loaf and place on a lightly floured baking tray. Dust top of loaf with flour and, using a sharp knife, cut a cross in the centre. Cover with a tea towel and leave in a draught-free place for 1½ hours or until doubled in size.

Preheat oven to 200°C. Bake loaf for 1¼ hours or until hollow-sounding when tapped on base. Cool on a wire rack.

White bread loaf

Makes 1 loaf

Don't get me wrong, I love a dense, chewy sourdough – but sometimes we all crave a slice of soft white bread, and there's nothing wrong with that. However, our options are mostly limited to the highly processed, additive-riddled options of commercial bakeries. This loaf may not last as long, but when freshly baked it satisfies all those cravings and more. It can also be a good way of giving kids what they want, so they fit in at school lunchtimes, before moving their palates onto something more robust.

2 teaspoons dried yeast
1 teaspoon sugar
525 g white bread flour
2 teaspoons fine sea salt
50 g lard or soft unsalted butter
olive oil, for greasing

In a small bowl, combine 60 ml (¼ cup) lukewarm water with yeast and sugar. Stir to dissolve yeast and sugar, then leave for 5 minutes or until yeast is foamy.

In a large bowl, combine flour and salt and make a well in the centre. Add yeast mixture and 250 ml (1 cup) lukewarm water, then combine with flour until a dough forms. Turn out dough onto a lightly floured board and knead for 5 minutes or until well combined. Add half the lard or butter and knead until smooth, then knead in the other half. Continue kneading for 10 minutes or until dough is smooth and elastic. Place dough in an oiled bowl and turn to coat. Cover bowl with plastic film and leave dough in a draught-free place for 1 hour or until doubled in size.

Knock back dough, then return to a lightly floured board and form into a loaf. Place in a lightly greased 20 cm × 10 cm loaf tin, cover with oiled plastic film and leave for 40 minutes or until doubled in size.

Preheat oven to 180°C. Bake loaf for 45 minutes or until golden brown and hollow-sounding when tapped on base. Turn out of tin and cool on a wire rack.

Cooking in a wood-fired oven

◇◇

One of the pride and joys of our kitchen is the wood-fired oven. Neatly tucked into a doorway that originally led into the corridor where children would line up for class, it was designed by Alan Scott, whose ovens are legendary.

While I was still living in Sydney I read a book Scott co-authored called *The Bread Builders*, all about masonry ovens and baking bread in them. So it was a serendipitous discovery when I learnt that Alan had moved to Tasmania, and this cemented my desire for one of his ovens. We were fortunate to meet the man himself and have his son Nick build our oven, which would turn out to be the last Scott-designed oven built during Alan's lifetime. However, his legacy lives on through the countless ovens of his design around the world and through those that continue to be built.

Alan spent the second half of his life honing the efficiency of the masonry oven through design modifications: the placement of each brick is carefully considered, with the ultimate aim of holding as much heat for as long as possible. This makes the oven a marvel to cook in, with incredibly even heat from front to back. To fire the oven to bread-baking temperature takes a full day and a full wheelbarrow of wood. The fire is lit directly on the floor of the oven, with the door left open to allow the smoke to escape. Probes throughout the oven allow the temperature to be constantly monitored, and when it reaches about 300°C, we often push the fire to the back of the oven and slide pizzas and flatbreads into the front to cook. When the wood breaks down into coals and the desired peak temperature is reached (around 500°C), the coals are spread over the oven floor and the door is closed, so that the heat suffuses the chamber.

The next day, the coals are removed, the oven floor is mopped out with water and the oven is ready to cook in. The heat declines slowly, enabling different foods are cooked. Higher temperatures are perfect for bread, particularly large, moister loaves of sourdough; the radiant heat is gentler than that generated by a conventional oven, and the oven holds steam, resulting in a fabulous crust. As the oven temperature falls, dropping to around 80°C over five days, it passes through the perfect temperatures for roasting, cake and biscuit baking, then slow-cooking and eventually for drying.

We cook everything from whole suckling pigs to soufflés in our wood-fired oven – it is the heart and soul of our kitchen.

Resources

I like nothing better than leafing through a cookbook, gardening guide or seed catalogue for ideas and inspiration. Listed below are some of the books and other resources I've found indispensable in our day-to-day life at The Agrarian Kitchen, and in the writing of this book.

General

— Maggie Beer, *Maggie's Table* (Lantern Penguin, Melbourne, 2005)

— Paul Bertolli, *Cooking by Hand* (Clarkson Potter, New York, 2003)

— Hugh Fearnley-Whittingstall, *The River Cottage Cookbook* (Harper Collins, London, 2011)

— John Seymour, *The New Complete Book of Self-Sufficiency* (Dorling Kindersley, London, 2009)

— Alys Fowler, *The Thrifty Forager: Living off your Local Landscape* (Kyle Books, London, 2011)

— William Rubel, *The Magic of Fire: Hearth Cooking* (Ten Speed Press, Berkeley, California, 2002)

Bread and wood-fired ovens

The late Alan Scott was a pioneer of wood-fired oven design, and his legacy lives on through the website ovencrafters.net, where plans are available, as well as information about having an oven built by Alan's son Nick, who built our pride and joy.

— Jeffrey Hamelman, *Bread: A Baker's Book of Techniques and Recipes* (John Wiley & Sons, Hoboken, New Jersey, 2004)

— Alan Scott and Daniel Wing, *The Bread Builders: Hearth Loaves and Masonry Ovens* (Chelsea Green, White River Junction, Vermont, 1999)

Home smoking

Domestic cold smokers can be assembled from simple materials: one of the easiest ways is to join an old firebox to a wooden barrel with ducting, cut out a lid in the top and place a hanging bar in the middle. There are many good books with designs galore (including the one below, which we used when we built our own smokehouse), so anyone with a backyard – large or small – can get smoking.

— Stanley, Adam and Robert Marianski, *Meat Smoking and Smokehouse Design* (Bookmagic, USA, 2009)

Growing

Although I grew up on a farm, I had little idea of how to grow food when we established The Agrarian Kitchen, so I've very much learnt on the job. The following books have helped me along the way, as has having access to an amazing array of heirloom and heritage varieties of fruit, vegetables and herbs.

— Steve Solomon, *Growing Vegetables South of Australia* (self-published, 2002)

— Eliot Coleman, *Four-Season Harvest* (Chelsea Green, White River Junction, Vermont, 1999)

— Roger Phillips and Martyn Rix, *Vegetables* (Pan Macmillan, London, 2007)

— Michel and Jude Fanton, *The Seed Savers' Handbook* (Seed Savers' Network, Australia, 1993)

Heirloom seed suppliers

Rangeview Seeds: **rangeviewseeds.com.au**
The Lost Seed: **thelostseed.com.au**
Phoenix Seeds: **phoenixseeds.net.au**
Southern Harvest: **southernharvest.com.au**
The Diggers Club: **diggers.com.au**
Eden Seeds: **edenseeds.com.au**
Four Seasons Seeds: **4seasonsseeds.com.au**
The Little Vegie Patch Co: **littlevegiepatchco.com.au**
The Italian Gardener: **theitaliangardener.com.au**

Heritage fruit tree suppliers

Woodbridge Fruit Trees: **woodbridgefruittrees.com.au**
Yalca Fruit Trees: **yalcafruittrees.com.au**

Acknowledgements

Without my family, none of this would have been possible. From the very beginning, my wife Séverine and son Tristan have been with me every step of the journey – I love you both dearly. Thank you to my mum and dad, for all the long treks down to Tasmania to help us when we were setting up in the early days, and to Séverine's mum and dad, for your support and eagerness to tackle any job thrown your way.

To my great friend Luke Burgess, your images are breathtaking. Thank you for your perseverance in making every shot special, even with everything else you had on at the time. Thanks for your advice and being a sounding board for the recipes – I always knew I was on to a winner when a dish was devoured as soon as the shot was taken!

I owe a debt of gratitude to the staff of The Agrarian Kitchen: without you, we couldn't open our doors. Thank you Rainer Oberle, for making the garden your own – I appreciate your dedication and enjoy seeing the garden constantly evolve. Thank you to Stacey Lewis, for being our right-hand girl in the kitchen and office, and for tirelessly cleaning up my mess during the production of this book – your enthusiasm is infectious. To Lee Farrell, a woman of many talents, from pottery to gardening, it is a pleasure to have you on board. Thank you to Jethro Havenhand – you seem to be able to turn your hand to anything, from pig wrangling to gardening and your latest incarnation as master brewer. Thank you also to Rhys Hannan, for all your hard work and help in the early days, and with the beginnings of this book.

Thank you also to the other teachers: Sally Wise, whose knowledge of preserving is a constant source of inspiration, Marcus Verney, my go-to man for all things meat, Linda Evans, your down-to-earth approach to home baking gives confidence to all; Graham Pritchard, who is always forthcoming with pearls of sourdough baking wisdom; and Alistair Wise, who I learn more from with each lesson he gives. Thank you, Alistair, for your friendship and generosity, and for your kooky sense of humour. Your child-like spirit keeps us all young at heart.

Thank you to Tammy, Donna and Sue at The Drill Hall Emporium antique store in New Norfolk, which became my unofficial prop shop during the shooting of the book. Thank you for your patience in letting me raid the store at inopportune times for the gorgeous and unique items that have helped make the photos even better. I am very lucky to have you so close.

Thank you to Mud Australia and Bison for letting me borrow props for what seemed like an age. Thank you to Charlotte Bell, for prop sourcing, which gave me the prod in the backside I needed to get this thing going. To Ben Richardson and Peta, my thanks and gratitude for making pieces specially for the book, and for location scouting and modelling.

My deep gratitude to the Penguin team: to my publisher and friend Julie Gibbs, thank you for having the faith in me to produce a book, and for sharing my vision of The Agrarian Kitchen and all it stands for. To my star editor, Alison Cowan, it has been wonderful to work with someone of your patience, humour and passion for food . . . and, of course, a fellow goat-lover. Thank you to Evi Oetomo, for your beautiful design work – your discreet touch is perfect.

Thank you to Tony, Sandra and Richard Nicholson, for welcoming me into your family. I treasure your friendship and look forward to much more time together. To John and Gwen Denton, the best neighbours anyone could hope for, thank you for everything – from your watchful eye to the rosemary I constantly pick from your garden. Thank you to Peter Cooper, for your knowledge of all things truffle and all the goodies we enjoy from your wonderful property. To Richard Weston, thank you for your enthusiastic attitude, and for being a constant source of garden inspiration and knowledge. Finally, thank you to the Lachlan community at large, for all your support. I feel truly lucky to live and work in this special part of the world.

Index

T

V

W

Y

Z

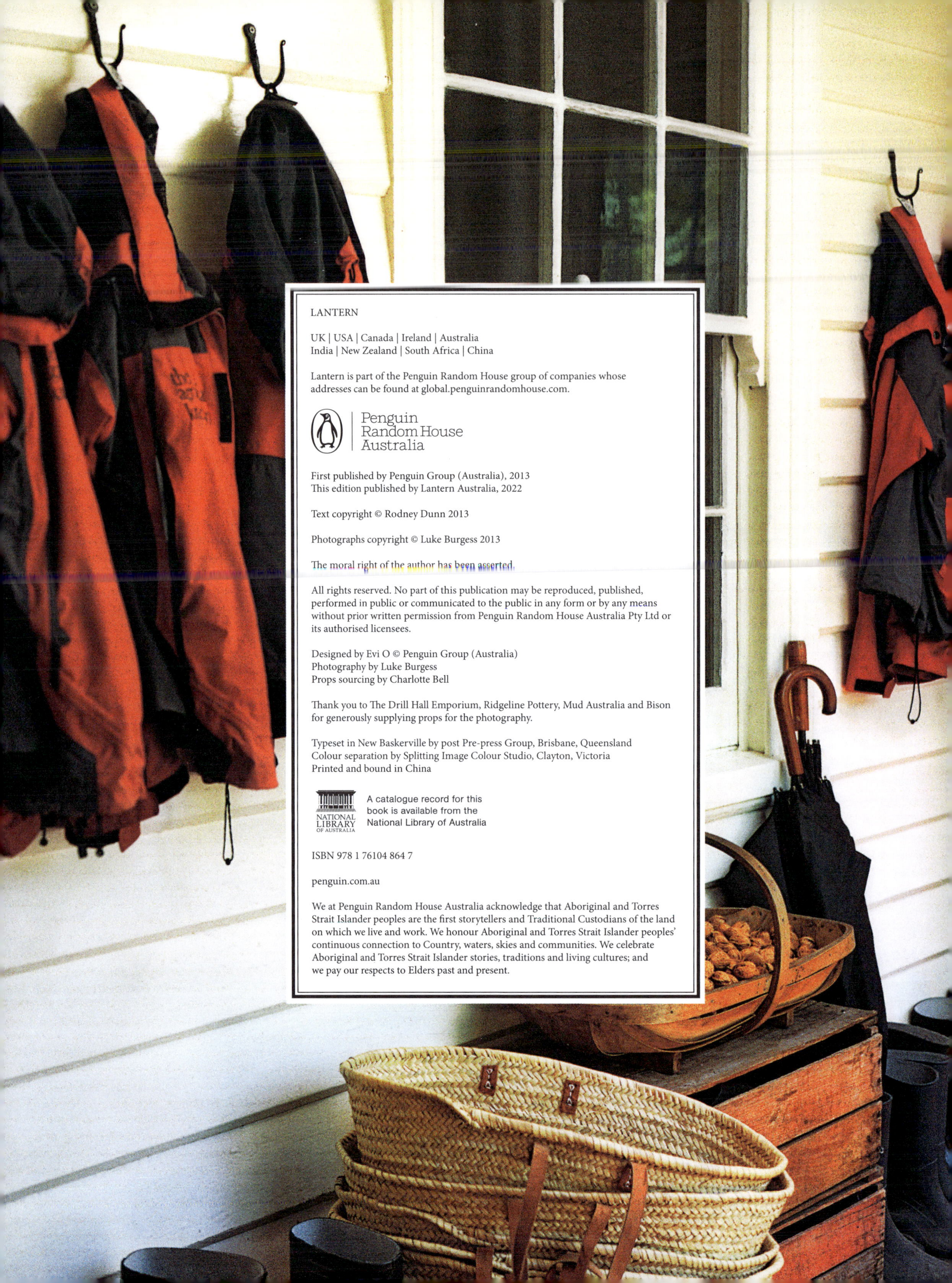

LANTERN

UK | USA | Canada | Ireland | Australia
India | New Zealand | South Africa | China

Lantern is part of the Penguin Random House group of companies whose addresses can be found at global.penguinrandomhouse.com.

Penguin Random House Australia

First published by Penguin Group (Australia), 2013
This edition published by Lantern Australia, 2022

Designed by Evi O © Penguin Group (Australia)
Photography by Luke Burgess
Props sourcing by Charlotte Bell

Thank you to The Drill Hall Emporium, Ridgeline Pottery, Mud Australia and Bison for generously supplying props for the photography.

Typeset in New Baskerville by post Pre-press Group, Brisbane, Queensland
Colour separation by Splitting Image Colour Studio, Clayton, Victoria
Printed and bound in China

NATIONAL LIBRARY OF AUSTRALIA

A catalogue record for this book is available from the National Library of Australia

ISBN 978 1 76104 864 7

penguin.com.au

We at Penguin Random House Australia acknowledge that Aboriginal and Torres Strait Islander peoples are the first storytellers and Traditional Custodians of the land on which we live and work. We honour Aboriginal and Torres Strait Islander peoples' continuous connection to Country, waters, skies and communities. We celebrate Aboriginal and Torres Strait Islander stories, traditions and living cultures; and we pay our respects to Elders past and present.